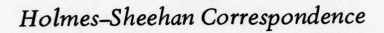

Holmes–Sheehan Correspondence

Other Books by David H. Burton

Theodore Roosevelt Confident Imperialist (1968)
Theodore Roosevelt, A Biography (1972)
Theodore Roosevelt and His English Correspondents (1973)
American History, British Historians (1976)

Holmes-Sheehan Correspondence

The Letters of
Justice Oliver Wendell Holmes
and
Canon Patrick Augustine Sheehan

Edited by

David H. Burton

National University Publications
KENNIKAT PRESS • 1976
Port Washington, N. Y. • London

Manufactured in the United States of America

Published by
Kennikat Press Corp.
Port Washington, N.Y./London

Library of Congress Cataloging in Publication Data

Holmes, Oliver Wendell, 1841-1935.
　　Holmes-Sheehan letters.

　　(National university publications)
　　1. Holmes, Oliver Wendell, 1841-1935.
2. Sheehan, Patrick Augustine, 1852-1913.
3. Judges—United States—Correspondence,
reminiscences, etc. I. Sheehan, Patrick Augustine,
1852-1913. II. Title.
KF8745.H6A48　　347'.73'2634　[B]　　76-22603
ISBN 0-8046-9164-9

For
The Law Alumni
of
St. Joseph's College
On The Occasion
of
The American Bi-Centennial
1776–1976

Contents

Preface

The reputation of Oliver Wendell Holmes, Jr. as a correspondent is enhanced by this edition of his exchange of letters with Canon Patrick Augustine Sheehan. Though the number of the letters is limited if compared with the correspondence of Holmes and Frederick E. Pollock or Harold J. Laski, this collection exhibits some unique qualities. Especially rich in elements of personal affection, these letters add significantly to what is, perhaps, a partially neglected dimension of Holmes—legal scholar, dissenting Justice, free-swinging intellectual. Catherine Drinker Bowen has made us fully aware of his tender love for his wife, while James Bishop Peabody in his Preface to *The Holmes-Einstein Letters* has described Holmes as "an essentially religious man." The Holmes-Sheehan letters bring these two strains together. By tracing considerations which were basic to Holmes's total personality, these letters suggest important influences in his public life as well as in his private relationships.

This edition of the Holmes-Sheehan Letters has been made possible by the scholarly perceptivity and kindness of a number of individuals. My colleague, Professor Raymond H. Schmandt, alerted me to the existence of the Holmes material in the Archives of St. Charles Seminary Library. Professor Grant Gilmore of the Yale Law School, the Literary Executor of the Estate of Oliver Wendell Holmes, Jr., has very kindly given me permission to make use of the letters written by Canon Sheehan which are on deposit in the Archives of the School of Law, Harvard University. At Harvard Law School the Librarian, Professor Morris L. Cohen, and the Curator of Manuscripts, Mrs. Erika Chadbourn, have been generous in ways great and small. Professor Cohen's permission to make use of the letters by Sheehan was vital to the whole enterprise. Father John Shellem, the Librarian at St. Charles Seminary, and the Archivist, Mr. Lawrence Taylor, have been no less considerate in giving me access to the copies of the letters written by Holmes which are part of the Heuser Papers at St. Charles Seminary Library. I am grateful to these individuals and to their institutions; the help forthcoming has always been informed by a sense of friendly concern.

In addition it is my pleasure to acknowledge the support of a number of others, including Mr. Daniel N. DeLucca, Vice President for College Relations, Dr. Thomas P. Melady, Executive Vice President, and Rev. Matthew G. Sullivan, Alumni Director—all of St. Joseph's College—and Sister Mary Beningus of "Canon Sheehan's own parish at Doneraile." I especially want to thank the members of the Board of Directors of the Law Alumni of St. Joseph's College and the President, Mr. John P. Quinn, and to invoke the memory of the Honorable Francis X. McClanaghan who first organized the Law Alumni. Without the interest and support of the Law Alumni the publication of these letters would not have been possible.

David H. Burton

Philadelphia, Pennsylvania
July 4, 1976

Holmes–Sheehan Correspondence

Introduction

The paradox of the friendship of Oliver Wendell Holmes, Jr.—American jurist—and Patrick Augustine Sheehan—Irish priest—is both apparent and real. Doubt and belief, "bettabilitarianism" and "faith of a Breton peasant's wife," man of science and man of God, the contrarieties existing between them can be variously rendered and honestly parodied. The letters which they exchanged over the course of a decade, 1903-1913, supply ample evidence of their conflicting attitudes and values. These same letters also reveal a sympathy, a tolerance, indeed, one must not hesitate to use the word, a love, each man bore the other. The paradox arising from the Holmes-Sheehan fellowship becomes a provocative one. The two friends did not merely agree to disagree on matters of common intellectual concern. Starting from different positions, often one hundred and eighty degrees apart, their intellectual propensities, their tastes, their moods frequently coincided. This common ground went deep, their friendship reaching the level of intimacy. The unguarded moments in their letters reflected this mutual affection, while occasional meetings in Ireland became meaningful reference points across the years of correspondence.

It was in Ireland that the friendship was struck. In the autumn of 1903 Holmes, while visiting Lord Castletown, who resided at Doneraile Court, Upper Ossory, County Cork, was introduced to Canon Sheehan. Sheehan was, at the time, the parish priest of the church at Doneraile. As his reputation stood high with Lord Castletown he met many of the important guests who came to stay at Doneraile Court. The Holmes-Sheehan friendship ripened naturally: they met and were soon at ease with each other. Holmes was probably surprised and certainly delighted by Sheehan's mind and manner. The Canon was a person of considerable erudition, a man of letters who was in the process of achieving something of an international reputation by his novels and his "reflections." On his part Sheehan was especially pleased that his new friend talked well on "philosophical topics," philosophy being one of the Canon's intellectual avocations.

Sheehan's origins and background promised but a portion of his life's achievement. Born in the parish of Mallow, near Cloyne, he was baptized on St. Patrick's Day, 1852. He attended the local National School and St. Colman's College, Fermoy, before entering St. Patrick's Seminary, Maynooth, in 1869. Ordination was followed by some years on "the English Mission" before a return to Ireland. The English experience had a considerable influence on Sheehan's manners and social sense, contriving to make him in ways an English gentleman-savant. But once back in Ireland, at Mallow, at the Cathedral in Queenstown of which he was made a Canon, and finally at Doneraile, his Irish heart reasserted in him a feeling for his native land. The result was an antithesis: the pious priest who read Carlyle and admired Pascal, the shepherd of souls who wrote novels full of psychological insights and trenchant comments on the Irish church and clergy.

Sheehan's concern for matters beyond the ken of the typical cleric of his day had manifested itself well before his years at Maynooth. He entered the seminary with an exalted ideal of the priesthood, from which he never wavered. He was equipped, as well, with a native intellectual curiosity which found nourishment in profane no less than sacred writings. Scholastic philosophy as it was dispensed at St. Patrick's, therefore, held little attraction. Instead Sheehan read Kant, Fichte, and Schelling, not to challenge the seminary authorities, but for the sake of the wider knowledge afforded. Many years after he left Maynooth he returned to read a paper on Spinoza which, he was told by one friend there, sounded "as a voice from unknown worlds." Sheehan's intellectual breadth, for example, enabled him to see in Pascal not merely a skeptic but a bold inquirer. In *Under the Cedars and the Stars,* his collection of reflections which so touched Holmes, he wrote: "When the Provincial Letters are forgotten or neglected as splenetic sarcasm and have passed away like the Junius and Drapier Letters, [Pascal's] Pensées will remain broken fragments of an incomplete but immortal work." Yet literature was perhaps Sheehan's truer calling. From Wordsworth, Shakespeare, Swinburne, Goethe, "the immortal Dante"—he derived insights concerning the human condition by traveling along paths known well enough to Holmes. In his productive years he concentrated on novels. Among the most successful of these were *My New Curate,* which gained a wide American audience, *The Blindness of Dr. Gray, Lisheen, Miriam Lucas,* and *The Queen's Fillet.* Though his settings for these stories were mostly Ireland, Sheehan explored human situations with sufficient psychological awareness to generalize his appeal and to gain an honest if modest reputation as a literary man.

Where Sheehan and Holmes tended to part intellectual company was in the latter's strongly scientific preferences. Educated liberally, but consumed by the study of law and its history, Holmes forever bore witness to his membership in the "Metaphysical Club" at Harvard in the late 1860s. William James, Charles Sanders Peirce, Chauncey Wright, and others along with Holmes were young thinkers with an enthusiasm for science which would promote the development of American pragmatism. As a result Holmes oftentimes rejected a priori notions in his quest for an understanding of the law. "The truth in the law," he observed in *The Common Law*, "is always approaching and never reaching consistency. It is forever adopting new principles from life at one end, and it always retains old ones from history at the other end, which have not yet been absorbed or sloughed off. It will become entirely consistent only when it ceases to grow." Nor was he loath to make use of the same judgments when it came to the meaning of life itself. Yet for all of that, Holmes comes through as a unique mixture of scientific imperatives and traditional values. He possessed his father's tenderness of spirit. He had known suffering while serving as an officer, thrice wounded during the Civil War, and came to believe in the nobility of sacrifice. Taking no stock in abstract rights, Holmes often resisted the amoral implications of Social Darwinism in his interpretation of the Constitution and of the law. As though to accent the larger dilemma of the scientific men of his generation he was fond of saying, with Madame de Staël, that while he did not believe in hell, he was nevertheless afraid of it. In contrast to Sheehan's secluded world, Holmes trafficked in large affairs. Weld Professor of Law at Harvard, Associate Justice and later Chief Justice of the Massachusetts Judicial Supreme Court, Associate Justice of the Supreme Court of the United States for thirty years, Holmes became distinguished, then celebrated, and finally revered as a public man. He was "the Yankee from Olympus" in the fullness of his years, 1841–1935, a perennial witness and a recognized prophet of the American experience.

Given the backgrounds and careers of Holmes and Sheehan there was no earthly reason why they need ever have met, and no ghostly reason why, having met, they should have become intimates. The strong temptation is to interpret their relationship as one of those strange, inexplicable attractions that are common to the human breed, a chemical bond, defying definition and stretching the poetic imagination, the temptation, in short, to avoid verbalizing the ineffable. Nor should the ineffability of the Holmes–Sheehan friendship be disregarded, however unsatisfying it may be in a final rendering of its nature. Only a reading of the letters yields an appreciation of the touching affection these two individuals felt for one another. From that reading one or more tangibles catch the eye. Holmes loved Sheehan's "tender, poetic, idealizing spirit," as he phrased it in one letter. He saw in the Canon a model for what was best in human nature. Sheehan in his writings, as in his life, spoke a wisdom which Holmes listened to attentively. Sheehan appealed to him much as Emerson had done in his youth, insisting on the "infinite worthiness" of every individual. It was as though Sheehan made alive and believable a world of absolutes which Holmes, the scientist, had ruefully dismissed. Sheehan, the man of God, was credible because he possessed the intellectual credentials Holmes deemed essential, yet he had, with his own peculiar genius, listened to the philosophers while remaining a saint.

If, according to the dichotomy of William James, Sheehan was a tender-minded soul whom Holmes readily admired, the Judge struck the Canon as a tough-minded intellectual who was a "regular Danton-Herod on paper and in theory," but was "not very hard hearted in practice." The priest was something of a master of disguises. After all, as any successful novelist, he was an acute observer of life who quickly penetrated Holmes's mask of scientific indifference to man's fate. Sheehan loved Holmes because he possessed the very attributes he counted as universal virtues: humility, resignation, courage, respect for ideals. An admirer of the *Autocrat of the Breakfast Table* long before the chance meeting of 1903, it was easy enough for him to love the "autocrat's" son. And, as in every true friendship, when examples multiplied of Holmes's genuine concern for his life and personal happiness, Sheehan could not but marvel at his friend's solicitude. "I grieve to think that you have days of pain," Holmes wrote in 1913, at a time when Sheehan was wondering if it was "right or fair that after a day's work, Judge Holmes should sit down and write a long and interesting letter to an old parish priest in a remote Irish village." Perhaps even the letters spell out the nature of their fellowship inadequately, and we are left to realize afresh that language can be a frail envelope indeed for conveying deep emotions.

The intellectual disagreements between Holmes and Sheehan were conflicts fully predictable. Nevertheless Sheehan elicited somewhat different responses to many basic philosophical questions than are generally associated, for example, with the Holmes–Laski dialogue. At the very least Sheehan was able to evoke from his friend a certain sympathy for a traditional understanding of the fate and purpose of man. Sometimes Holmes was prompted to express himself merely in negative terms, as when he wrote of mysticism as a willingness to believe that one's own ultimates need not be the cosmic ultimates. Yet one cannot believe that concessions to the "old verities" were made out of respect for the Canon's religious convictions. He was too intellectually rigorous to resort to such a ploy. A more plausible assumption is that Sheehan stimulated in Holmes a residual traditionalism. To be sure, this was a feeling more faint when it came to ultimates than can be discovered in some of the jurist's Supreme Court decisions which sought to protect both the individual and society from ancient injustices. His admission that man may have a cosmic destiny beyond his ken, Sheehan appears to have extracted largely because of his own serene faith in God. To such a faith Holmes did not remain impervious even though, as he once remarked, he could not believe it except by a "total collapse" of his scientific conceptualizations.

The letters written by Holmes and Sheehan are not full of intellectual combat. While differences between the two friends surface regularly, the moderation of the argument overrides the argument itself. The significance of their correspondence remains the affection, sometimes brought forth in the most tender way, that grew between the judge and the priest. It reached a climax toward the close of the Canon's life, with each man conscious that Sheehan's time was close at hand. Though the initial meeting at Doneraile in the fall of 1903 must have been a delightful interlude, Holmes's reading of *Under the Cedars and the Stars* seems to have cast a spell upon him, which he often acknowledged. Just as Holmes was drawn to Sheehan, the Canon ardently desired the Judge's friendship—"a source of permanent and unalloyed gratification" as he was to write in an early letter.

The succession of letters shows that Holmes was anything but anxious to use his friend's beliefs as a philosophical sounding board. Nor was Sheehan hot on the trail of an infidel who yet might be saved. Each man accepted the other for what he was and what he stood for. Much of the charm of the letters rests upon this consideration as the friendship unfolds. To listen to Sheehan say: "I have come up from the sea, where I spent three happy weeks, my summer holidays, . . ." for example, is to become aware that all the writer of such words wanted was to share some part of his memories with a friend separated from him by miles of ocean. While Holmes, in turn, would discourse on his judicial responsibilities dealing with something as prosaic as a patent case because what he really desired was to "sit down with you in your dear well remembered place and you with me in this library which I think you would like. . . ." There are no armies of ideas clashing on a darkling plain in these letters. Rather there is to be discovered the sunlight of toleration and, yes, of love. The total Holmes is differently viewed and better understood because of that.

Students interested in the "mind and faith" of Oliver Wendell Holmes, Jr. must be thankful to Rev. Herman H. Heuser, the friend and biographer of Canon Sheehan, for the preservation of as many of the letters of Holmes to Sheehan as have survived. A perusal of the letters in sequence shows that some letters are missing: undelivered, lost, or neglected. Readers of Heuser's *Canon Sheehan of Doneraile* may be surprised in fact that any corpus of letters written by Holmes is extant in any form. Heuser recounted in his book how a few days before his death Sheehan burned the manuscript of his Memoirs "as they might do harm to others." That his entire collection of letters and papers was not consigned to the flames does not seem improbable. Furthermore, Sheehan wrote to Holmes in the June before his death that Holmes's letters had been "carefully filed and kept to be disposed at your pleasure when I have gone." Holmes apparently believed the letters he wrote to Sheehan had been destroyed upon the Canon's death. It seems likely that these letters were in fact disposed of, but not before Fr. Heuser was able to make copies of the bulk of the letters written by Holmes to Sheehan. The letters included in this volume are verbatim copies of the transcripts available in the Archives of St. Charles Seminary Library and in the Archives at Harvard Law School. Few, if any, handwritten originals exist and it is difficult to determine if any matter has been omitted or spelling or punctuation revised.

Heuser began work on his biography of Sheehan in 1914. In his book he made use of the Holmes–Sheehan correspondence. When the time came to publish *Canon Sheehan of Doneraile* Heuser consulted Holmes in order to verify the accuracy of those passages in the book dealing with Holmes. The jurist's reaction to Heuser's enterprise was twofold. In November, 1916, he wrote Heuser after reviewing portions of the manuscript: "I am disturbed to learn of the existence of my letters. I sometimes wrote confidentially and always with the freedom one practices to an intimate, expecting no other eyes to see them." But when the finished biography arrived, Holmes was much pleased. "The life of Canon Sheehan has come," he informed Heuser in November, 1917, and "surpasses even my expectations . . . a beautiful memorial." In the pages that follow, the letters of Justice Holmes and Canon Sheehan written with a moving sense of brotherly concern become their own memorial—*in pignus amicitiae*—to a rare, warm, and instructive friendship between an American jurist and an Irish priest.

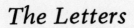
The Letters

Doneraile, Co. Cork
December 19, '03

Dear Mr. Holmes,

I have received and read your speeches,[1] since I wrote. Accept my thanks for the pleasure they have given me. My sympathies were altogether with the "war" and "academic" speeches. They are full of that fire and vitality that go to make real eloquence. But I think your "law" speeches were a greater triumph, though I could not read them with the same sympathy. But to command the dry bones to rise up and be clothed, as you have done, was a Prophet's work.

Why have you not gone into Congress, where you would have a much wider field?

With all good wishes for the N. Year,

I am, dear Mr. Holmes,
Yours very sincerely,
P. A. Sheehan, PP.

I had no idea that you had gone through the Civil War. When will its real history be written?

On December 27, 1903, Judge Holmes wrote in part:

This is the first time since I received your gift that I have had a chance to open a book. . . . Today there has come a breathing space and the first thing I took up was *Under the Cedars and the Stars.*[2] I am greatly and unaffectedly charmed and moved by it. . . . But I did not start intending even to hint at any controversial thought but simply to express to you my appreciation of the beauty and loftiness of your thought and of the song of the words in which it is clothed. . . . I am afraid my pleasure will be rather onesided. But it is genuine and my admiration sincere.

On January 2, 1904, Judge Holmes wrote in part:

This is just a postscript to my former letter to say that I love your book. . . . I am as far as possible from being on your side—but I still hope you will have room for a little pleasure when I say that your book moves me more intimately by old world feeling than anything that I have read for a great while and that if you did not regard me as an enemy I think it might be that we should recognize each other as friends.

The next month, February, 1904, Judge Holmes wrote again:

At the risk of wearying you I write once more. This moment I have finished your book. It is the only book, except for a few short light things that I don't count, that I have read since I received it. . . . And now I must tell you once more of the love and exaltation which your words have the skill to command, as few words that I have read anywhere can. It is true that I don't believe your philosophy—or shall I say, the religion you so beautifully exalt. . . . But I love an idealist—even while I doubt the cosmic significance of our judgments. . . . When I begin to write to you I am tempted to say many things, but I refrain. I do not want to burden you either with my reflections or with the feeling that you must answer. I simply want to tell you more emphatically than before now that I have finished your book that I owe you my admiration and thanks.

Doneraile, Co. Cork
3. 2: 04

Dear Mr. Holmes,

I am very grateful for your generous appreciation of my book. You have been much before my mind these latter days. On reading over the book for corrections and index, I stumbled across one or two expressions and thought with a little qualm of regret: "Judge Holmes, I fear, will be grieved at this." Then a paper came to me from Taunton, Mass., with your portrait and some account of your entering your new house.[3] Then finally came your letter, containing such a nice expression about my book.

Would you let me assure you that there is no antagonism between us? We differ in our interpretation of human life and the universe around us; but that fact, so far as I am concerned, in no wise diminishes my esteem for you. I respect your conscientious convictions; nor have I any right to intrude within the sacred sanctuary, where each soul is alone with God. Conscience is the supreme monitor. I would that all men believed as I do, for I believe that this faith is not only the solution of what is otherwise inexplicable, but also the great proof and support of the human soul under the serious difficulties of life. But I have no right to force this conviction on you; and the fact, that you see with other eyes than mine, should in no way imperil or diminish the friendship, which I take the privilege of assuming, should subsist between us. I assure you I esteemed it a great kindness on the part of Lord Castletown[4] to afford me an introduction to you, first, for your good father's sake, whom I have learned to love from his kindly, human writings, and then, for your own.

I am a great believer in the words of S. Paul: "There remain faith, hope and charity; but the greatest of these is charity." I have toleration and friendship for all, but one class—the aggressive and intolerant. You might read this in my book. I think that any one that deliberately hurts another, in feeling or person or property, is very much to be reprobated. Life is such a tragedy to so many, that any one who seeks to accentuate its trials, is unworthy of human fellowship. We have one supreme obligation —to be kind to each other. And I must say, that is the spirit of my Church today. In the past, things were different all around. There is a new spirit in the world today.

But I can not regard with equanimity the efforts of nonbelievers to destroy the faith of the masses by scoffing and proselytising their disbeliefs. Hence although German rationalists have done a great deal to destroy Christianity, they have approached the subject at least with reverence unlike the wretched French, so closely imitated by modern writers who ridicule what they are incapable of understanding; and dishonestly destroy the great prop and support of a tottering race. That class of propagandists raises my anger; and yet perhaps even there, there is pity too.

See how much one word in your letter (*ever again to be eliminated*) has drawn from me. I assure you that your acquaintance was a pleasure; your friendship a source of permanent and unalloyed gratification. I have

[13]

just space to wish you many happy years in your new home.

Very sincerely,
P. A. Sheehan

Later in the same month, February, 1904, Judge Holmes wrote:

Your letter came this morning and gave me the greatest pleasure. My most constant associate among our judges is White,[5] a Catholic, and the other day when I was speaking of the logic of persecution he agreed but said we, none of us live logically—you (Holmes) professing skepticism act on dogma; and those who profess dogma do not and could not carry it out dogmatically—the spirit of the times is too strong for us. . . . The C. J.[6] hinted at sending me a case to write as I am a man of leisure. I like to read a little philosophy to purify my palate, like an olive after lunch, and when I can get a moment's time I love to write to a friend. . . .

Beverly Farms, Mass.
September 6, 1904

My dear friend,

There is still nearly a month of vacation ahead of me before I go back to Washington and I don't like to let it go by without a little talk with you. I remember hearing Emerson say once in a lecture, "The lover writes 'Meet me at half past seven precisely without fail. I have nothing particular to say. Thank God.'" I have nothing particular to say and so I will give you a short account of my life since I last wrote. The last term of the Court was interesting. I wrote some judgments which I was glad to have a chance to write and I think I am succeeding in my new place. The most exciting one in a popular sense was the Northern Securities Case,[7] which caused me some pain at the moment, as I was compelled to express an

[14]

opinion contrary to what the President ardently desired. The newspapers were full of stories of his wrath, etc., but he is all right and the incident is closed. I say it caused me some pain in the sense that it is always painful when you run against what a personal friend is hoping for and perhaps expecting. Of course such considerations have no effect on the mind of one who is accustomed to weigh questions impersonally or who is fit for his business. . . . I have been unusually well this last winter and this summer and have a happy feeling of resting from work in anticipation of beginning to work again. Don't forget me—but remember that I always am sincerely your friend. . . .

Doneraile, Co. Cork
Sept. 29, '04

Dear Mr. Holmes,

There must be a sympathy in facts, as well as an association in ideas, for just as I got your letter of the 6th inst., you were brought to mind vividly by a picture of the house at Cambridge where O. W. Holmes was born; and by a quotation in the same magazine from Paul Bourget, which runs thus:

One of the most eloquent of the magistrates of Massachusetts, Judge Oliver Wendell Holmes, Jr., has said in one of those short speeches so full of soul, in which he excels: "Even if our mode of expressing our wounds, our awful fears, our abiding trust in face of life, our death, and of the unfathomable world has changed, yet at this day, even now, we New Englanders are still leavened with the Puritan ferment."

Then Lord and Lady Castletown[8] are here just now; and I have heard that you have written. So all around you occupy a pretty space in my thought these days. If I can not write all I think, set it down to the fact that I have just returned from a brief holiday in Germany, and that there are six inches high of letters before me.

I am very much pleased to learn that you feel as thoroughly well after your years of labours; and refreshed by your holiday for new work. I consider your office an extremely arduous one. At least it would be so for me. In all my mental processes, the one that affects me most by its strain upon the mind, is the balancing of facts and arguments towards the formation of a judgment. Strange to say, I can give free rein to the imagination for hours together without the slightest fatigue. And I can concentrate my thoughts on a process of reasoning, although I find this distressing. But to weigh and balance, and judge—that is an ordeal I always avoid when I may. I am sure you don't feel it so; partly because you are trained to that habit of thinking, although your extraordinary powers of eloquence are mostly associated with the imaginative faculty. But I can conjecture what mental anxiety you must have suffered in the case you mentioned, where you had to face the dilemma of maintaining your judicial integrity and the possibility of displeasing friends. These are the things that make grey hairs, even while they elicit and develop all that is wholesome and virile in a man.

About Plato. I lean much towards him. I do not care for Aristotle. He has too little fancies and too many facts for me. And after all, I am every day becoming more and more convinced that the best of our thinking is done with the heart and not with the brain. Yet, Aristotle is one of the Saints of our Church. St. Thomas has built his stately pile on his shoulders; and the Aristotelian philosophy is the foundation of all Catholic theology. But, all my own predilections lean towards idealism rather than realism, towards St. Augustine rather than St. Thomas; towards Plato rather than Aristotle. Hence, I am utterly unqualified to be a judge, or a bishop. If I were the former, I should leave all discussions to a jury; if I were the latter, I would put my crozier in Chancery.

Arnold[9] and Clough,[10] whom you dislike, are two of my favourite poets. I think the latter very much overpraised and the former very much underrated. But I feel a curious pleasure here in my safe retreat, where problems of life do not touch me personally, in going out and experiencing that strange melancholy that seems to be characteristic of our times, and of which these two poets are perhaps the best interpreters. I suppose it is the same feeling that makes one listen to the storm and the rain on a wintry night, when one is safely housed, and the curtains are drawn and the fire is bright, with a peculiar, and almost selfish pleasure. But I can read all Arnold a hundred times over when I can not touch Tennyson.[11] He seems to me to have felt more deeply. I can not dissociate Tennyson from my idea of an artist, who is always aiming to be out "on the line."

I had a pleasant three weeks in Mannheim, Germany. All that a good government, solicitous for the progress of its people, could do, has been done for this charming place. And the people!—a calm, grave, courteous people, enjoying life without noise or excitement, and infinitely polite to each other and to strangers. I could not help thinking of my own poor country, where everything is so tragical and sad.

Keep well; and do not deem me impertinent if I say, hold fast, as you have always done, to the great principles of justice and truth, so often controverted and repudiated in these days.

Always and most sincerely
my dear Mr. Holmes,
P. A. Sheehan

Washington
October, 16, 1904

Dear Father Sheehan:

When the work has begun I suppose we both are too busy to be able to write much or often, but I must just tuck in a line, especially apropos of your exhortation at the end of your letter, which moved me affectionately. . . . I am often struck, in talking to my wife, whom I greatly revere, with the power of a great sweet moral nature to sweep one into dogmatic affirmations, like the dogmatic affirmations of our tastes. But I tell her the free intellect will have its smile—and the last word is to him who can explain. Which I don't expect you quite to agree to and say not by way of controversy but just to tell the natural bent of my mind. . . . This is not entitled to an answer for months. But some day when you are at leisure, if you ever are, and are remembering me as I hope you sometimes do, remember that I wrote you last.

I forget to say that I am with you down to the ground about Tennyson. I call it stall-fed poetry—and when I want to be unpleasant to Britons I airily advert to persons as at the Tennysonian stage of culture. He was a man of genius of course, but when you come to those who came after him, those who share the peculiar exquisiteness which we know in modern society—and who only hope that some day they are going to be something particular, or not even that—the Lowell school as I imagine them. And yet some of the cleverest men in England seem to have looked up to Lowell.[12] I used to say that they made one set of reputations for home and another for foreign export.

Beverly Farms, Mass.
Sept. 17, 1907

My dear Canon:

I must write a line to you, now that I am quietly as home, were it only to tell you two things—1) that my servants were delighted at the things that you gave me for them—I told them they came from you; 2) that some talk led me to surmise, or rather I should say, suggested that your drawing or engraving was a first sketch by Millais[13] for a painting of his. I should think this probable. The face of St. Stephen is too subtly drawn not to be by a modern; and Millais is strong on subtle facial expression. I had a quiet voyage home on the sober-sided Boston steamer with a sober-sided lot of passengers—so having no temptation to frivolity I fell to improving my mind and read a French work on the routes pursued from the hypothetical starting points in the great plateaux of Asia which created the different social types according as they have been by mountain, desert, or sea, etc. I also read a work on the early Greek Religion—which is interesting and would be more so were it written by a man with a purely matter of fact straightforward style. It is written by a woman, and has a kind of Ruskin [14] and Swinburne[15] and water flavor. The epithets smack of factitious emotion. There is too much of the "lovely" for a shilling—and other things that would not worry my coarse hide as "ugly" etc. When she comes to deal with some of the details which modern taste regards as indelicate, she rather shrinks and dodges. Still the book is instructive—though I find Salomon Reinach[16] more amusing. It makes me a little sad to be led to believe that the hatred of Capital is widespread with us. All the natural laws seem to be set down to the discredit of the rich and people who would not dare to blaspheme are ready enough to damn Rockefeller or Morgan. Meantime I incline to believe a magazine article to the effect that before our clamorers for 8

hours (with which clamor I rather sympathize) know it, the Chinese
with their endless gluttony for work, their honesty and their imperturb-
able patience will cut the white races out in the markets of the world.
However I did not sit down to write a dissertation, but to send you my
love and my hopes that you will not forget me. I write from Beverly
Farms, Mass. but expect to be in Washington, D. C. not long after you
receive this. I am going to try to idle and rest for a few days, but I am
conscious of a sort of anxious uneasiness—I don't know exactly why.
Today is the anniversary of Antietam[17] where I was shot through the
neck, 45 years ago. I always think of you with affection.

Doneraile,
Co. Cork
Oct. 5. '07

Dear Judge Holmes,

I had followed you in spirit across the Atlantic, with all hopes that
you would have a prosperous voyage; and I was much gratified to receive your letter and to learn that your passage, if dull, was quite un-
eventful in dangers. I am also greatly pleased to know that your domestics
were gratified by the little gifts we were able to send them. I sincerely
hope that this has been by no means your final visit to us; but that you
will find time during the long vacations to run over again and give us
the great pleasure of seeing you. For your little morning visits to me
were gleams of sunshine across a grey and monotonous life; and I look
back to them with pleasure, but also with the regret that such experiences should be so transient. I think I mentioned to you that I felt my
greatest want to be some intercourse with minds whose ideas would act
as a stimulant to thought, by casting new lights on old subjects. And,
although we agreed to differ on many points, it was very refreshing to me
to be brought face to face with original thinking on the subjects that are
of deepest interest to myself.

Lord Castletown has not yet returned. He has been very busy in
Scotland and at a Pan-Celtic Congress, where the six Celtic Nations were
represented, and which seemed to be most interesting from an international

standpoint. I see that he is now engaged in the commission for the re-afforestation of Ireland—an admirable idea, if our conservatism would enable us to carry it out. There is a great deal of zeal and energy just now expended by all classes on the promotion of Irish industries too, but the headway they are making is not apparent.

I don't like that last sentence in your letter about your feelings of "anxious uneasiness;" although I am quite certain from similar experiences that it is a passing sensation, probably the result of your sea-voyage. But I like very much your very kind and generous expressions of friendship, which I beg of you to believe, are most cordially reciprocated.

I am ordering my publishers to send you the first copies of two new books of mine—"Lisheen"[18] and "Parerga."[19] This latter is the 2nd series of "Under the Cedars and the Stars."

Always faithfully,
P. A. Sheehan

Washington, D. C.
November 7, 1907

My dear Canon,

I thank you so much for sending me your novel.[20] It has the same sweet idealism, the same poetic turn that I know, the same tender feeling. I wish that I had something to send in return—but I fear that a few timely words on *res judicata* or on the police power of the States might not give you the same pleasure. When I got back I stopped at a hotel in Boston and was talking with a waiter I knew and telling him I had been in Ireland, County Cork. He asked me if I had been in the neighborhood of Doneraile. I said yes. Whereupon he asked if I had seen Canon Sheehan. It seems that he was a reader and admirer of your works. Every little counts. And as an admirer is the vehicle of truth, it matters not that he is humble. I am working so hard that I don't often get a breathing space before dinner and afterwards I find it wise not to read or write. Therefore I have read your novel by snatches—ten minutes at a time. I think your fashionable people and men of the world are not quite so real as your peasants, and I wonder whether there is not implied too wholesale a condemnation of the fashionable world. And yet just before your novel came, I was saying to some one that I rather thought that if the fashionable world of America (excluding those people of power who happen to belong to it but do not derive their distinction from belonging to it) was destroyed by pestilence, the world would be better off on the whole, and that I surmised the same of England.

But if it is true, I don't hold that opinion from any particular radicalism, but rather because the function of fashion is to furnish standards, and I do not see that it performs that function in any very valuable way in your country or mine.

In spite of my occupations I have read a short little book by Petrie the Egyptologist[21] —a biting bit—on the *hard* side, which I also favor as against the apotheosis of failure in modern sympathetic literature. Oh, I am a regular Danton-Herod on paper and in theory. I am not very hard hearted in practice. I dined last night at the Brit. Ambassador's[22] and met Sir Anthony—who is it? the deputy boss of Ireland at the Castle —but only had a word with him.[23] My friend, Mrs. Green admires him much. Do you? And do you know Mrs. Green?[24] She also has ideals and humor, and an Irish tongue . . . but I am willing to take the risk of that. Well I must dress for dinner. I have sat my 4 hours in Court and had a morning's rest, and generally have one after two hours on getting back— but this pen has been slack and so I have had a chance to talk to you, as one is tired out at the end of the day.

Ever sincerely yours,
O. W. Holmes

Washington, D. C.
March 21, 1908

My dear Canon:

Again you make me love and admire your tender poetic idealizing spirit. I received your *Parerga* two days ago and last night I read the first part, with some little peeps ahead. It is charming and I am very much obliged to you for sending it to me. It is strange how little the difference in our point of view prevents my sympathizing with what seem to me your dominant feelings and attitude. . . .

Well, I will pass to other themes. I have been working away under the usual high pressure and therefore have done a good deal more writing than reading. . . . At odd moments I am reading Gibbon, more because I suppose I ought to before I die than for any great nourishment I get from him. He is easy pleasant reading enough, but I don't care for general history—that written by literary men. The interest of history to me is the relation of cause and effect and such writers know little of real causes. It is different with histories of economics, law and philosophy. In them one really can see something of a real process. We are about to adjourn for two weeks, but as I have kept my cases written up, I don't see how my work can fill my time and hope to improve my mind a little with books and walks in the country. The spring here is more enchanting than I have known it elsewhere. A week ago Sunday I passed a birthday. I am 67. I try to realize that the prospect is short, but as you say, the present is more vivid than our imaginings. I still feel strong and well and take keen delight in my work. But I hope I have contemplated the end enough to meet it with composure. I don't think it desirable that one should do more and withdraw energy from one's tasks to meditate futilely on something else. In this same way I like to alter the paradox (I dare say I have to you): that a sense of responsibility is a confession of weakness. If I put all my powers into deciding the case and writing my decision, I neither feel responsibility nor egotism, nor yet altruism—I am just all in the problem and doing my best. This letter does not justify its length except as an affectionate reminder from—

Yours sincerely,
O. W. Holmes

Beverly Farms, Mass.
August 26, 1908

My dear Canon,

It is a year since I have heard your voice or seen your handwriting and as I think of you often I hope you will like a word from my quiet summer to remind you that I still exist and have not forgotten our friendship. . . . I shall be here through September—but already Washington looms a cloud on the horizon. Happy though I am here, there is my most vivid life. Meantime I have bought a two-thirds interest in the place that I spend my summers in, to avoid the risk of being turned out and rather expect to buy the other one-third before long. It is a little place near the sea where we have our summer outfit and can find it convenient and pleasant to return to. I wish I could see you in it. In the mornings I generally read and write and in the afternoons my wife and I take a drive in the woods where automobiles can not go. I play solitaire and get 8 hours sleep, drink little or nothing and try to accumulate strength for the 8 months high pressure of my Washington work. I hear occasionally from L. Scott[25] whom I brought to call upon you. He is succeeding wonderfully, as he deserves, for he is one of the most faithful of men. I hope you will be glad to hear from me.

Doneraile, Co. Cork
Sept. 11, '08

Dear Mr. Holmes,

Yours is one out of two or three handwritings, which, when I recognize on an envelope, gives me a thrill of pleasure and compels me to leave my breakfast cool until I read it. The vast bulk of my correspondence I put aside until I have leisure; and some letters I should like to have the privilege of never opening. But, though I am always hoping that you will buy a typewriter—no, that's not true, for then I should miss the personality that shines through your letters—I always tear your envelopes open, and I put you in my red arm chair and listen to your delightful monologue.

I have come up from the sea, where I spent three very happy weeks, my summer holidays, and where I saw sunsets and moonrises that would make a poet even of a politician. Of course, you haven't our glorious skies over there; and yet I can imagine from that little bit of description, which you allow to creep into your letter, that your woods and seashores must have an inexpressible charm for a mind that must be on the strain for eight months of the year. For if I am to judge by my own feelings, I think no mental effort uses up so much brain-power as the balancing of judgments, and the agony of making a right solution between conflicting arguments. I read some of your judgments lately in "The Literary Digest"; and I said what strenuous thinking that means. After all, the poets have the best of it. They touch the spring of their aeroplanes and are off into the empyrean.

The British Association[26] have come by one. Lord Castletown had an idea of bringing some of the learned ones down here; but I think they were surfeited with Dublin hospitality. There seems to me to be some bathos in these scientists waltzing around a ball-room, or talking platitudes at a five o'clock tea. But I suppose Homer must nod, or go to sleep altogether. But there was not a single paper of even slight importance read. The scientific papers threw no new light on the mystery of things; and your department of political economy was hardly touched.

How that terrible question of "socialism" is looming up! There is starvation amongst the workingmen of Glasgow, and riots, Prince Arthur insulted, etc. I have just seen one good word for democracy and the future in a volume I have just put down, where it is proven, that in your democratic America with all its progressivism and levelling down, reverence for women is increasing. The thought had not struck me before.

Have you taken up as yet the great book I expect from you? With such a style as yours (although it could not be popular) and such ideas, you ought to give the world a memorable book.

I am just commencing in the "American Eccll. Review"[27] a story called "The Final Law" in which I try to preach if I can not prove, that above the iron laws of the Universe there is a higher command; or, as Tennyson puts it: That Love is Nature's Final Law.

> Always affectionately
> P. A. Sheehan

Beverly Farms, Mass.
September 21, 1908

Dear Canon Sheehan:

I have the advantage of you, as my vacation is not quite over and so I write at once on reading your letter, if it were only to tell you the real joy it gives me to receive your kind and affectionate words. Don't let my swift return bother you with any feeling of obligation. I know what it is to be busy, and soon after you get this I shall be in the whirl myself. I hope to be in Washington Oct. 7, after a few preliminary days in Boston and New York. The vacation has gone by in a flash of quiet. On the 17th I drank a glass of wine (contrary to my custom when I am alone at home) to the living and the dead, it being the anniversary of Antietam, where, 1862-1908—46 years ago (!) I was shot through the neck. It is 6 years since the yesterday when I went to Washington. Time goes quicker as one nears the Fall. My latest amusements have been Scribe's[28] plays which I translate aloud to my wife of an evening after a game of solitaire. . . . I was interrupted in the middle of the last sentence to drive with my wife—it is getting cool for driving in the afternoon. We went to a little graveyard that goes back to the 1600s. I copied this to send you "Col. Benja Marston lies here, who died May 22nd 1754 —being 57 years and 3 mos. old—Art thou curious reader to know—What a sort of man he was. Wait—till the Day of final retribution—& thou mayst be satisfied." That "retribution" sounds ominous, as to his neighbors' opinion of him, I meant to tell more about my last subject, but I will shut up—just sending my love and every good wish, along with the appreciation you know.

Your affectionate friend,
O. W. Holmes

Bay View Hotel
Ballycotton, Co. Cork
June 13, '09

My dear Judge Holmes,

I am here for a quiet holiday above the eternal sea—that same sea that washes the shores beneath your delightful villa. It needs no violent stretch of the imagination to picture us shaking hands across that little span of waters. But as fancy will not make things possible, I must only use the penny post to send you greetings, to hope that you keep well after this labouring session, and to thank you for the three printed copies of your legal decisions which duly came to hand, but which I have hitherto failed to acknowledge.

I was much interested in these judgments, although it is not easy for the lay mind to follow the intricacies of legal arguments; and the balancing of the three elements—justice, reason, and precedent, which seems to me a most difficult task. I often wished that you could see a very remarkable treatise, "De Legibus,"[29] written by the Spanish Jesuit, Suarez, and in which lately I have been again interested as I have had occasion to refer to it in some writing. It is a ponderous folio volume of about 750 pages, double column, closely printed; but it is a masterpiece of close, consecutive reasoning, and as such, is a monument of industry and intellectual power. It has never been translated into English; and like so many other vast treasures, it lies locked up in medieval, but correct, Latin. I often wonder, why legalists have not heard of the book. They would burn Coke[30] upon Lyttleton[31] and all other commentators.

This is an antique, out of this world, Keltic and fishy village, just enlivened by the presence of a half a dozen Londoners, who come over here from the smoke and fog of Babylon, to inhale some sweet air, and to exercise man's great privilege of destruction by killing all the fish they can, out upon the deep seas. It is not for food they kill but for "sport" —to be able to say in a London club: "I killed a skate, weighing 125 pounds, and several hundred conger eels." It reminds one of Teufelsdrockh's Epitaph on Count Zachdarm in "Sartor":

Quinquies mille Perdices
Plumbo confecit.[32]

I hope the Water will waft you to Doneraile in the Autumn.

Always most sincerely
my dear Judge,
P. A. Sheehan

Beverly Farms, Mass.
July 17, 1909

Dear Father Sheehan—Or Canon ought I to say?

Your letter met me here on my return from England—a return
without seeing you! But they wrote to me from Oxford this year offer-
ing me the hon. degree of D. C. L. so I flew over, took it, was taken
[photographed] in my gown and cap to prove that I had worn them,
and flew back again after a few days in London. I meant to write to you
from there, but was in such a continual hurry that I got no chance. I
was pleased with the honor, though such things make less impression as
one grows older. One reasons and accounts for things and the result is
that very few hit one where one lives, if you will pardon the slang. Only
the recognition of the competent counts. To be sure this degree has that
element in it, but one wonders whether one does not owe it partly to
the personal friendship of some of those in power. However I don't know
who those in power are, and will try to get a modest swagger out of it.

Of course I know the name of Suarez and you tempt me to get
hold of him, but my time is so much occupied that I doubt [I shall].
You will not quite share my point of view, but I regard pretty much
everything, and especially the greatest things, in the way of books, as
dead in fifty, nowadays in twenty years. The seeds of thought germinate
and produce later seeds. The old structures are remodelled and have elec-
tric lights put in. One of the proofs that a word contains living thoughts
is that it kills itself. So, I know, a priori, that no one who wrote in the
16th, 17th, or 18th century will say the poignant thing I want. He will
not have the historic sense, he will not have the *philosophy* that seems

to me vital. I'd read him [Suarez] as I read Montesquieu, simply to admire his genius. I said in an introduction to the Esprit des Lois that to read the great men of the past was the last achievement of a studious life. You see I talk from the point of view of one who thinks that philosophy and the philosophy of history really have advanced within quite recent times, and specifically that the law, although lawyers are apt to be behind the times in their science, is known and studied in a far more profound way today than ever before. If I privately think I have done my share to help such a result, that is merely the illusion of personality by which nature gets our work out of us. I have something of the sporting feeling left in me, and I think that perhaps this age has overdone its unwillingness to face or inflict pain. But I find as I grow older that I am much inclined to agree with you in dislike of seeking pleasure at the expense of any kind of life. I am afraid, however, that I should like to catch a tarpon and also a salmon or two!

I find among the books waiting for me one by H. G. Wells on America.[33] He seems to have had the penetrating thought of trying to find the ideals of the country. I doubt if he found them. I doubt if there is yet such consent and unity as to be capable of formulas. I do not feel sure of nationality as a basis. All I can think of to do is to pound away producing one's best and not to lie awake nights with cosmic worries—having taken the faith to believe that the world is not my dream and that I am not running it. —Dear Father Sheehan, you don't mind my levities, I hope, knowing the sincerity behind them, a sincerity that includes affection for you.

Doneraile, Co. Cork
August 31, '09

My dear Judge Holmes,

If you were now in Washington, gowned and ermined, and trying to maintain judicial equanimity in an atmosphere of 94 degrees or so, I would not inflict a letter on you. But, seeing that you are happily in undress, and with no responsibility beyond the ordinary human duty of killing time, and strolling on pebbly beaches, and driving through fragrant pine-woods, I can not forego what is to me a very great pleasure indeed, —namely, to congratulate you on the distinction lately conferred on you by the Oxford Dons.

The fact has raised these latter gentlemen somewhat in my esteem, because it seems to indicate that they have departed from what has been a religious tradition in the British mind, that everything American is very "young" and immature, and still under the benevolent patronage of the mother country. Only quite lately in the "Times" literary supplement, some letters of Swinburne's were published, in which he speaks in a very patronising manner of your Emerson; and again, quite lately, I have been reading the letters of Coventry Patmore in which he ridicules the idea that Longfellow could ever be considered a poet. And I send you herewith a copy of the supplement (Times) in which you will notice a certain tone of British condescension towards American litterateurs, whilst accepting the world's verdict on the "Autocrat."[34] When, therefore, Oxford found *you* out, I am beginning to respect the English intellect a little, and to think that in their own elephantine manner, they are being spurred into line with the thinkers of other nations.

Only yesterday, your name turned up in Doneraile Park. Lady Castletown mentioned that you had been over; but I think they regretted they had not seen you, or that you were unable to visit. Lord and Lady Castletown were much pleased with the Oxford affair.

To drop down to my humble self, I am sure you will be interested to hear that some good priests out in Australia want me to travel 12,000 miles, and to spend the rest of my life with a mitre (far weightier in every way than your wig) governing an immense diocese under a tropical sun. Of course, Rome is too wise to listen to such a suggestion; and I have been selfish enough to use all the machinery I could avail of, to prevent the possibility of such a thing. So I take it as a pretty French compliment and nothing more. But these are the little accidents of life.

I do hope that the Centenary celebration of your revered father will be the success every lover his books and [his] gentle character expects.

The leaves are beginning to turn here; and our Indian summer is commencing. I suppose you will soon be in the Forum again.

Always most sincerely,
P. A. Sheehan

My dear Canon in esse and Bishop in posse.

I am equally glad in my turn of the appreciation of you, and on the other hand rejoice that you don't want to go so far afield. For I assume that if Rome knows what is good for her the time cannot be far off when you will be offered some place nearer home, and I should grieve that the uncertainty of our meeting again should be turned into an impossibility, unless indeed you travelled by way of Washington or Beverly Farms.

I saw the Castletowns as I flitted through London, but alas I saw Ireland only from the Cunard decks. I don't know how well you remember Leslie Scott, whom I brought to call upon you—his wife is with us now for a little rest and we three, Mrs. Holmes, Mrs. Scott, and I walk and drive and talk, and if she isn't bored it is due to her affection and my wife. Certainly she gets rest. The result is that I read no more Law and Philosophy but only lighter matter aloud.

Fourteenth. I was interrupted yesterday and I am glad of it for I see that what I said about you might seem as if I were taking a politician's view of a spiritual office. It is so hard to make sure against giving wrong impressions at a distance. I know and appreciate the spirit in which you approach such questions, but as, of course, I do not believe the same things, I naturally think more of your advantage than of anything. I do not know whether you have the faculty of administration, which must be necessary for success, but I should wish to see you relieved of the labors of a parish priest. There must be places in the Church that would give more unhampered scope to your gifts. I do not know enough to have definite desires and hopes, so perhaps it is best that I simply should wish whatever you most would like to befall you. That, I certainly do. In a little more than an hour I have to go to Boston for the night, in order to attend a dinner to the President, much against my will. I have not been notified that I shall be called upon to speak. If I am I shall say but a few banal words. I don't think it desirable that our Judges should talk much off the bench, although one of them does, much to my regret. Also I have nothing I want to say. I took part in a local show last Saturday that was different—a review of the veterans of this county by the President at Beverly. I was a guest of the soldiers and was in the procession. From 1000 to 1500 old fellows with faces twisted by age and work, but alive with the romance of their memories. The march was only a mile for we are getting old. I was moved as I always am when I see a lot of them together and could but think that every year now the line would shorten a good deal. I began to realize what when I was a boy I used to think [it] would be a fine thing—to be carried in a civic procession as a survivor. I little thought of what it was to be a survivor, then. Well, I must stop this rambling talk. It will convey affectionate etc.

Washington, D. C.
November 19, 1909

Dear Canon:

Your new book[35] arrived yesterday and I read the first three chapters last night. They make me love you, like all that you write. I thank you sincerely for sending it to me. I am in my work up to my ears. At this moment I am deep in a patent case. The State Courts have no jurisdiction over patents so I never had much to do with them before I came here and they only come up to us occasionally by permission for some special reason, so I am having a somewhat new experience. I like all kinds, however, and shall try to talk as if I had waded in physics all my life; knowing very well that the party I decide against will say that I know nothing about it and don't understand, which I flatter myself that I do. I wish that we could realize the fable of astral bodies and alternately I sit down with you in your dear well remembered place and you with me in this library which I think you would like.

Affectionately yours,
O. W. Holmes

My dear Canon:

It would be ill to let the summer go by without reminding you of your heretic friend. I am especially turned in your direction by having read last night an article in the *Atlantic Monthly* by Father Benson interpreting the signs of the times as showing that the future belongs to the Catholic Church.[36] I shouldn't be surprized myself, if I knew that the opposing force would be not Protestantism but unbelief, but naturally I do not attribute the same importance that Father Benson does to Chesterton and his Olive Lady. .

I have lost a dear friend in the death of the Chief Justice.[37] I wish the President would appoint White (as he would not think of me, who am White's junior.) Of course I should like the place, although I never have thought of it as a possibility,—but place doesn't make a man's work any better, and my only ambition, I can say without a hint of the least mental reserve, is to do the best work that can be done. I have been interrupted in the most unexpected way by the reporter of our decisions turning up and taking me for a motor drive. I stick to a horse and a quiet jog through the woods so that I can see and hear. Those space devouring rushers over the earth give me little pleasure, and now that I am here, I must stop again to go to the post office with a letter to a man who wants to be heard about a Chinaman who has been denied entrance to the country. . . .

You don't mind, I hope, my running on, and popping out with anything that happens to come into my head as I write. Our friendship is sincere enough to exclude reserves that hamper freedom. Of course, I don't mean to obtrude differences—but consciousness of them sometimes suggests lines of thought that might not occur to one if one were writing to a different man. I wonder what you are doing meantime. I believe I told you that my wife wanted me to go abroad mainly that I might go and see you— but I told her I didn't want to leave her and would not go unless she would join me—which she would not. As one gets older the anxieties of distance increase. I forget whether I told you of my experience last winter with Dante. I found that Latin and French enabled me to construe the Italian easily with the help of a translation and I read him through—the great poem that is—and had the greatest literary sensation of my life—much to my surprize. I will not run the risk of repeating what I may have said—further than to say that the intensity of his spiritual rapture expressed in divine song moved me through and through. I have lived in a dream, although the law seems remote from such raptures—and it has seemed to me that it was a dream of ideals—although I am well aware of the elements of personal ambition to excel—to do better than others—I have taken the loftiness out of it. . . . Well, goodbye. I send this with some fear that parts of it may strike you as better omitted, but I will take the risk.

Affectionately yours,
O. W. Holmes

Doneraile, Co. Cork
August 26, 1910

Dear Dr. Holmes,

You are very much in my mind these last few weeks, probably because of the Autumn holidays or perhaps it was a presentiment of your letter for which I was craving. The great want of my life is lack of intellectual intercourse; and your letters are a stimulus that drives me from the superficialities of daily life into depths of thought where I have no temptation otherwise to plunge.

I think Fr. Benson's forecast of the future of the Church in America is not altogether chimerical, although probably his reasons for thinking so are quite different from mine. Whether America is yet in its adolescence, or whether it be the result of climatic conditions, there is a certain buoyancy and delightful optimism in the character of the nation that is very much akin to the Catholic spirit. And there is also depth of feeling and generosity which the older nations have long since cast aside in favour of the "critical spirit." All this tells in favour of the Church; and I think if some great thinker could reveal the inner serenity, and sense of security, with the occasional raptures that belong to certain choice spirits, particularly in our cloistered communities, half of America would rush away from the fever of modern life, like the anchorites of old, and bury themselves in monasteries.

Would you be surprised to hear that in what you say about "intellect," you come very near the dogmatic teaching of the Church, especially as revealed in the late Papal Encyclical against "Modernism"[38] —one of the most remarkable documents that has ever been issued by the Holy See? It is a condemnation of "emotionalism" or "intuitionalism," as the sole motive of faith. The Church takes its stand upon reason as the solid foundation on which Faith rests. Hence its approval of the Thomistic philosophy, which rests entirely on the syllogism, a view accepted also by John Stuart Mill. But, as you say, intellect has its limitations, which we are all painfully conscious of; and, therefore, if we are to reach Truth, there must be some other avenue. This we call Faith. For after all, if Intellect is the supreme and final Judge of Truth, the question at once arises, whose Intellect? or what condition of Intellect? Is it the Intellect of one solitary thinker, like Aristotle, or the common intellect of the "man in the street"? or is it the intellect of an Aristotle or a Bacon in his youth, or in his manhood, or in his old age?

I have just been reading "The Autobiography of Herbert Spencer." He appears to have modified, at the age of 60 or 70, half his dogmatic teachings as a young man. Age, experience, illness, imperfect circulation of the blood in the arteries of the brain, impure blood from hepatic troubles —all these were elements that modified half of his conceptions during life. What then? Well, it follows that if we accept "intellect" alone as the norm and standard of truth, we drift at once into the belief that all knowledge is relative, and there is no absolute truth. This won't do! And it is here the intense logical consistency of Catholic teaching comes in. The Absolute Mind alone can discern absolute Truth. The moment you speak of limitations, or say "we cannot know," you admit that. Therefore, what we can know about the Universe, is just what reason verifies and what Absolute Truth has *CHOSEN* to reveal.

Why do I underline that word? Because, such is the pride of human intellect, that what we are really in revolt against is—the Reticence of God. We forget our place in the Universe, because we have never got rid of that Geocentric Theory which makes the little microbe, man, the apex of the Universe. We have to be humble, if we are to aspire; and we have to accept with thankfulness the little and yet the great deal, that the Absolute Mind has chosen to reveal. We, Catholics, believe that that revelation has been made to the Church; and it is the only Church in Christendom which asserts that and speaks with authority. You think that therefore the Church is bound to coerce and persecute. Certainly not. First, because to coerce conscience by punishment is totally opposed to the spirit of the Church on the sole ground that is a fundamental principle of Catholic theology that "the end can never justify the means." You will lift your eyebrows at this; and say: What about the "Provincial Letters," and "Jesuitism," and all that? But, I am only stating the literal truth, no matter how Catholic doctrine has been twisted and abused by men. There is no more fundamental principle in all Catholic ethical teaching, so much so that one of the most familiar questions in our daily catechising of children, and in our Sunday preaching is:

"If by one lie you could liberate your father from prison, or release all the souls that suffer in Purgatory, would you be justified in uttering it?"

And the answer is: "No! No object, however holy, can justify a thing that is evil in itself."

I know you will not urge mediaeval persecutions which we all condemn and deplore. The ages were barbarous; and then heresy was a political crime, a kind of treason—felony when the Church was identified with the State; and when heresy was productive of many social evils. —No one finds fault with the Versaillais troops for shooting down the Communists who set Paris on fire.

Besides, the spirit of our age will not tolerate persecution, altho' the *Kulturkampf* of Bismarck is rather recent. Advanced education will kill all that.

I send a little volume on the attitude of the Church towards animals. You will see how hopelessly wrong Pierre Loti is![39] Have you seen Huysman's "En Route"?[40] The story of the swineherd Simeon is unique—a mixture of ecstatic rapture and daily and hourly contact with animals that makes me sick. But it is "Catholicity" undoubtedly, in one aspect, though it is an aspect that does not appeal to me.

I am in thorough sympathy with you in your conviction of the sacredness of human liberty. It seems to me a kind of sacrilege to trespass on that Holy of Holies—the human conscience. Hence I have been for the last few months here in Ireland in a state of silent fury against the insolent domination of the Irish Parliamentary Party and their attempt to stamp out all political freedom. At last, I was forced to speak, and I send you two articles on our political situation, and in favour of a new movement to establish political liberty and break down the barriers between Protestants and Catholics in this country. But, whilst I would resent any attempt to interfere with my principles or convictions in political and social matters, or to restrict my freedom in any way, whenever the Eternal speaks (and every day I am becoming more overwhelmed with a sense of His Omnipresence) either through direct inspiration or through the Vicariate He has established on this little planet of ours, I am a little child; or as Pasteur said: "I have the faith of a Breton peasant; and, if I live much longer I shall have the faith of a Breton peasant's wife."

You will smile at all this. No matter. You see what Dante thinks. I know from what you have said that you. . .have seen the glories of the *Paradisio.*

We have had disastrous weather here. Eternal rain. Not a glimpse of sunshine any day; but sheets of rain. The harvest is ruined.

The Castletowns are here. Lady C. is only recovering from a serious operation on the eyes; and Lord Castletown is not so robust as usual.

The infirmities of age are creeping down on myself and I am becoming more home-tied every day, working on and trying to get in as much useful travail as I can before the night falls. It would be the rarest of all pleasures to see you; but you are right to economise your strength, and yield to the physical inertia which your mental expenditure induces.

With all respect for my co-religionist, I do most sincerely wish that my next letter shall be addressed to the Lord Chief Justice of the States.

> Ever sincerely
> my dear Dr. Holmes
> P. A. Sheehan

Beverly Farms,
Sept. 3, 1910

Dear Canon:

I must have another whack at you while I am here, were it only to thank you for your dear letter, the fine articles, and the very interesting book. But I must do justice to Pierre Loti—he does not speak of the Church but of the Gospels. . . .

Sadness comes with age—or ought to, I suppose. I sometimes try to force myself to feel worse than I do remembering that my next birthday will make me 70. When you speak of infirmities and my friends here die, I really do feel gloomy, but my interest in life is still so keen, I still want to do so much more work, that in the main I feel pretty cheerful. Especially candor compels me to admit when I am led to think that my work is valued as I should like it to be—and here you will discern the [vanity] I am afraid —but as I believe I said I meet him [death] with a grin and cut under him by recognizing that vanity is only a way to get any work out of me, and that my only significance is that which I have in common with the rest of things, that of being part of it.

Supreme Court of the
United States
Washington, D. C.
March 1, 1911

My dear Canon,

There are many things to write about and I wish I could talk with you. In the first place your book came two days ago or so, and I have read about half of it with much pleasure and shall read the rest before the week is out. There is so much that I sympathize with and that shows your delicacy and high feeling. Also I like the poems—you have increased your mastery of poetic expression, if I may venture to say so, since the little volume you gave me. I chuckle a little in one beautiful stanza at your Irish—"The jasmine dropped one pear(ru)l from her hair." Your discourse as to science I think but a half truth, though I have seen similar thoughts emphasized in a book sent to me by Fred Pollock[41]—Keary, "The Pursuit of Reason."[42] I think science has changed our point of view, and for the better. But there I touch controversy. Also I think there is a contradiction in your seeming opinion that our tongue gains by its infusion of Latin and Greek and your exaltation of Old German, which seems to owe its quality to its sticking to Latin roots. . . .

There are more things that I want to say but I hurry on. Do you know anything about the Castletowns? I know that they have had reverses and I gather that he has collapsed, but I can't ask Lady Castletown questions, and I don't know exactly what it means. Will they come no more to Doneraile? On that hypothesis I was discussing with my wife the possibility (I doubt the actuality) of running over to Cork and coming up to see you for a day and returning. Naturally I have been very anxious about the C's but I have heard very little, which makes it worse. . . .

I think we should not have had a controversy about the Classics if the language had not been taught as if every boy were intended for a pedagogue. One might learn to read Latin or Greek as I did German, enough for literary purposes, without all the bother about rules learned by heart etc., etc., in a very short time. I do think a great deal of time has been wasted—and I do think that a rational understanding of one's personal environment, so as not to expect the interstitial miracle, is part of a true education. Oh I have lots to say, but I am scribbling off this letter before going to Court and have to hurry. I was deeply pleased that Berlin gave me a degree last autumn—I mean as deeply as anything of that sort can please me—for I could not explain away the surprize by friendships, etc. On the 8th of the month I shall be 70. I mingle sadness and satisfaction—and send you my love—my friends die—and time brings you closer to me.

Affectionately yours,
O. W. Holmes

Doneraile, Co. Cork
March 25, 1911

Dear Dr. Holmes,

I hardly expected that you would find time from your judicial work to cast your eyes over "The Intellectuals:" and I am greatly pleased that you did not dislike the book. It would be expecting too much that you should give it the "Index" *Approbatur!* because I know that you think in a complex and involved manner, whereas this book had to deal with platitudes, and I am afraid in a way too transcendental for the multitude, and not academic enough for the truly learned. I intended it to be an *Eirenicon* between the rather furious parties into which Irish life is divided; but here again I am not over-sanguine, because the book will not be read except by a few, whose tastes and sympathies have already placed them beyond the zones of political antagonism. It is an unhappy and distracted country and the one thing that hitherto saved it,—a certain kind of Celtic idealism—has now given way before the advances of materialism.

The Castletown affair was very tragic. Lady C. has undergone a painful operation for the eyes in London; and was but partially relieved. They had returned here, and then the crash came. So unconscious was Lady C. that any danger impended, she had spent £400 in erecting a new Hall in the village. Her grief was pitiable; and so was Lord C's remorse. He had sold out all the *purchased* estates; and had speculated wildly (so it was said) in foreign investments, which proved useless. Receivers were at once sent down here to take charge of everything. Lord C. is at Granston; Lady C. in London. I understand they are allowed £2000 each per annum; and the latest news is, that the estate was not so involved as was at first supposed; and that possibly, they may be able to return at no very distant date. Meanwhile, Sir John Arnott, who has rented the place for the last few years during the hunting months, has now taken over the Court for 12 months. One of the sad things connected with the affair was the destruction of the entire herd of deer in the Park. During the autumn, all day long we heard the crack of rifles in the Park. They wrapped the venison in the hides and sent all along to the London market. The one agreeable feature was the universal sympathy awakened for Lord and Lady C. especially for the latter. It was very touching.

I must not fail to congratulate you on your new degrees.[43] The two leading universities of the world have now said: Well done. It is a fine verdict on your three score years and ten.

I suppose you will run over for the Coronation in June, If you can get the glitter out of your eyes and submit to a little Irish greyness and boredom, there is one at least who will be more pleased at seeing you again than you can well imagine. I am just entering my 60th year; but I have no long lease on life. I am only anxious to get in as much work as I can before the night falls.

> I am, dear Dr. Holmes,
> Always affectionately,
> P. A. Sheehan

I am taking a liberty in sending you by Book Post this evng. my own copy of "Dante"—the companion of my holidays. I have unfortunately made pencil marks here and there; they will only amuse you. It is a pretty portable edition; and perhaps it has not reached your side of the Atlantic. Don't trouble to acknowledge; but keep it *in pignus amicitiae.*

Supreme Court of the
United States
Washington, D. C.
April 1, 1911

Dear Canon:

You bet I will acknowledge your letter and book. If I ever had seen
the latter I should have bought it at once, as it is the most convenient and
delightful edition I have ever come across, and the *pignus* and your letter
warm my heart. As to coming over, the Coronation would do more than
anything else to keep me away if otherwise I expected to come. What
would bring me would be the wish to see my friends—not least, yourself.
But as I have told you, I grow more unwilling to risk the ocean between
my wife and myself so that I hardly think that I shall do it unless she will
come with me—but I prophecy with the uncertainty that comes from the
knowledge of her ingenuity when she makes up her mind that it is better
for me to go.

I read your Intellectuals through, of course, and loved its tender spirit
and generous recognition of souls outside your faith. I have just heard a
strange tale of one within it. My classmate Kent Stone, a grandson of
Chancellor Kent, a famous man in his day, began as an Episcopal clergyman,
married and had children—his wife died, he became a Catholic—gave away
his children—and went to South America, as a Trappist I believe. He came
back here and I met him as Father Fidelis, a man of the world and seemingly
learned (he was one of the two first scholars in the class). Yesterday, I
went to the funeral of another classmate—Emmons, a distinguished geolo-
gist, and I was told that a letter had just come from Stone, saying that he
was returning to South America to pass the rest of his life in penance—
bidding goodbye to us all and requesting that Emmons should write to him
no more. How strange to compare the different schemes of life. A man who
probably by current standards has lived with more than ordinary virtue,
goes away to solitude and penance. Another, but there is no need to work
the [scheme] out. On the other side, one cannot but wonder whether such
a life does not exhibit a kind of spiritual egotism. To sacrifice one's obvious
duty to one's children, for instance, and as I believe happened, though I
may be wrong, commit them to belongings inferior to those in which they

naturally would have grown up—well, I think there are moral problems that may be solved either way—that life is painting a picture not doing a sum, as no doubt I have said before, and that to get certain effects others must be given up. I remember hearing the tale of a man whose father died deeply in debt after having been supposed to be rich—the son was married. He gave up his profession, took to something that gave him a small but certain income, spent his life in paying his father's debts and in consequence condemned his children to a lower place in the world. He chose honor as Kent Stone chose sanctity—at whatever cost to others. I neither approve nor condemn, but simply accept a possible solution as one among others.

Oh my dear Canon you are lonely, but so am I although I am in the world and surrounded by able men—none of those whom I meet has the same interests and emphasis that I do—barring those elements common to all who are trying to solve the same problems and do their duty. I am speaking too only of my work, but that is two thirds of my life. Outside of that my wife has made my whole life a path of beauty. She has a real genius, I say it advisedly and confidently, and has devoted all her powers to surrounding me with enchantments. So that when I say I am lonely, I feel bound to confess that it is egotism—the feeling thrown back on oneself when one sees little attention given to what one thinks most important. I am rather ashamed of my outburst but I shall send my letter as I have written it. The frame of mind that I am afraid I often am in and express is little better than one you would deem sinful. I look at a man as a cosmic [insignificance], having neither merit nor demerit except from a human and social point of view, working to some unknown end or no end, outside himself and having sufficient reasons, easily stated, for doing his best. But I am powerfully moved by the opposite view as Dante shows it, and I rather shudder at Newman's[44] suggestion that a man may be highminded, honorable, etc., and yet find himself classed among the enemies of God. I am as likely to believe the Roman law to be the law of today as to accept your faith, but we are apt to see our merits as physiological but our failures as sins, or at least find it easy to do so. I love your marks upon the 3 vols. They gain a new value from them. I fear that this letter is a discourse, and only semi-articulate, but it will tell you that I am truly grateful and affectionately yours.

O. W. Holmes

Dear Dr. Holmes,

I received your Harvard speech[45] and the kind words accompanying it. It has one fault. It is too brief; it compresses too much into too narrow a space. But perhaps I am judging rashly of Harvard intellects. Such an address should be diluted into twenty pages over here, before it could be fully grasped. I underline the following for future reference:

1. "For I own that I am apt to wonder whether I do not dream that I have lived."

2. "The 20th never wrote about itself to the newspapers."

3. "To hammer out as a compact and solid a piece of work as one can, to try to make it first-rate, and to leave it unadvertized."

4. "Life is painting a picture, not doing a sum."

5. "In the very heart of it there rises a mystical spiritual tone, that gives meaning to the whole."

6. "Our only but wholly adequate significance is as parts of the unimaginable whole."

7. "While we think we are egotists, we are living to ends outside ourselves."

How cordially I can agree with all this—and yet with what different eyes we look at the same thing and draw such different conclusions. I perceive this is what you mean when you say, *Life is painting a picture.* But I won't accept that. It sounds too like the subjective Idealism of Fichte. There must be objective truth somewhere; and all questions in religion and metaphysics run to this: where is objective truth to be found?

Now this little crossing of swords is all your fault. You achieve in your brief lines, what I have always been anxious to achieve in larger spaces, i.e., you provoke controversy. The best compliment that can be paid to an author is to challenge him; and I want to know what are "the ends outside ourselves." I could never appreciate Tennyson.

> There lives more faith in honest doubt
> Believe me than in half the creeds.

for:

> And one far-off divine event
> To which the whole creation moves.[46]

There! you have stirred up the Celt!

You will have received "The Queen's Fillet"[47] by this time. I think I have been impartial. But nothing can convince me to adopt the new theory that Robespierre's atrocities may be condoned because he was *just about* to do better things.

I have been reading again all about Beverly Farms, north side of Massachusetts Bay; the villas perched on cliffs, or nesting by the shore; the broad beach; and the man who carries with him everywhere three wounds suffered in his country's service, and "*unadvertised.*" They are not the least factors in the profound esteem and affection of your Irish friend. You will notice how tenderly I have handled Talleyrand—because he put France before the world.

> Always affectionately
> my dear Dr. Holmes
> P. A. Sheehan

> Beverly Farms.
> August 14, 1911

Dear Canon,

It is a relief to hear from you for I was beginning to fear that you were not well. Not that I had any reason, except an occasional expression in your letters, but just the fear that comes after a certain time when one does not know. Your book I shall not see until I get to Washington, as all books sent there remain at my house—& if there were any way to instruct a negro messenger who can't read I should order it sent on—but I don't dare attempt the experiment. But perhaps you directed it to Bev. F. If so, it has not come yet. As to your notes on my little speech I must answer one or two points. As I must have said before, all I mean by *true* is what

I can't help thinking, and I define truth as the system of my limitations. . . .

The other day as I was reading Fairfax's translation of Jerusalem Delivered, I noted a thing to mention to you.[48] Fairfax is Elizabethan—(1600, the introduction says) and he uses "pearls" and similar words as dissylables, i.e., "Whose shells great pearls. . .pour out," i.e., pear-els. Cant 17, stanza 23. I may add that I got unexpected pleasure. He has a streak of poetry that is his own and his originality strikes me as less rococo than C———————* and having not much more magic and miracle than Tasso believed. . . .

If I thought the Powers would take any pleasure in the oriental prostrations taught by a religion brought from the East, I would crawl on the floor mighty quick you may be sure.

Do you know the poems and letters of Thomas Edward Brown[49] — the poems are Manx and very full of human feeling and the letters I think among the few that are worth rewriting. When you say I have aroused the Celt in you, I grin with joy—though you don't give me a real whack on the head—but it reminds me of what Lady Alice Gaisford once wrote me, that a friendship wasn't cemented until you had quarrelled—although we are still a good way from having done so. I am afraid you idealize Beverly Farms—though it is a pretty place, and the contours of the ground, thanks to glacier action I am told, are noble. So that a rocky rise of 30 feet, black with hemlocks, gives a suggestion of the sublime in small; and there are long windswept downs (I think you would call them) a little inland, that have a little sublimity of a different sort. But the cliffs are minuscule as compared with Ireland, which really fills the demands of one's heart as one sails along the coast. My little acre has some rocks in it of which I am proud, and which I love—for the Beverly rocks are my first recollections of country—and what we love and revere is largely determined by our earliest memories—n'est-ce pas? I enclose a hideous little photograph of my house; the two windows are of the room where I am sitting and have a glimpse of the ocean. . . . I must turn to less agreeable tasks—so goodbye.

Affectionately yours,
O. W. Holmes

* Word not legible.

My dear Canon,

Here we are again, after a lost June. We were kept in Washington
later than usual, whether because the Chief Justice forgot that 100 days notice
was necessary before adjournment or because he wanted to get some cases
disposed of, I don't know. But the result is that I am just beginning to feel
settled, and the first thing I think of is to write to you. I can't do it while
I am working. After getting here the next week was broken up by my having to go to Williams College in the western part of the State to take a degree. It is a lovely place. The College is like a citadel upon a high hill surrounded by mountains and remote from the world. It is a center of
Congregational Orthodoxy, the starting point of the foreign missions from
this country, I believe. (I see you smile, and naturally I kept some of my
opinion to myself—looking at them as the champions of a lost cause—the
final issue being between you and me.) The whole impression was sadly
charming. I heard with delight the bobolinks singing as they hung in the air
over the mountain meadows. I made a little speech. It did not sing, as I
like to have them, but I took the chance to fire off some of my economic
opinions—that most people think dramatically not quantitatively; and that
the sentimental socialism now more or less in vogue is based on the dramatic
contrast of the palace of the employer and the hovels of the workmen, etc.
not on a consideration of how much is withdrawn from the total by the
palaces and fine domains. I said that I was informed that 85 percent of
the total product here and in England was consumed by people with not
over $1000 (£200) a year—the whole expenses of government and the
moderate luxuries of the many coming out of the remaining 15 percent—
that if there was a real fundamental economic wrong it must be proved by
proving the figures wrong, not by contrasting the rich and the poor, and
that the real public evil of the extravagances was that they reenforced the
dramatic fallacy—from that point of view they are a social crime. I believe
all that, devoutly, and for twenty or more years have been saying it and
expressing my wonder that those who had the chance and the duty did not
press it home before it was too late. But alas although what I say is platitudes, I find them habitually overlooked and forgotten on all sides. It is
not popular to tell the crowd that they now have substantially all there is,

and that the war upon capital is the fight of the striking group against all the other producers for a larger share of the annual product that is divided among them. As long as people stop with questions of ownership or money and don't think of the stream of annual products and who consumes them, they are sure to think fallacies. But I have let my pen run away with me. I want to know how you are, and what new expression your beautiful spirit is finding. As for me I have not yet begun to read. But this morning a New York correspondent, I am not sure whether a crank or genius, who has a vision of a new government arising outside the formal limits—e.g., the N. Y. Clearing House, etc.—sent me a book on Proudhon,[50] alas in German, which I don't read easily. I gather that P. had more of the future in his head than most of the others—but I shall see. What a refuge your religion is from the terrors of the universe. I could not believe it except by a total collapse—but it must be a joy and warm up the interstellar spaces. Also at present, of course, it gains great strength as a representation of law and order. I was struck by a parade of the Knights of Columbus in Washington the other day. How it had turned potential toughs into respectable upholders of organized society. Well, this is only a [message] of affection, though I have rambled, and an inquiry if all is well with you.

Your affectionate old friend,
O. W. Holmes

South Infirmary, Cork
October 6th, 1912

Dear Judge Holmes,

My brother forwarded your last kind letter of inquiry to me; and, altho' not convalescent (for that would imply recovery, and recovery with me is out of the question), I am able to satisfy one desire, that of letting you know how grateful I am for all your solicitous inquiring. Two years ago a Dublin surgeon diagnosed some internal trouble, and left no hope of cure; but I went on working until a sudden collapse came in June, which brought me to the gates of death. To my intense disgust and regret, the doctors pulled me back from the "eternal rest" to face the world as a chronic invalid. I have hopes of leaving here, and perhaps of resuming some parochial work; but life for me is henceforth to be carried on on a broken wing. Fortunately, I have no pain; and no depression of spirits whatsoever. But I wish I had been at rest.

The words "regret and disgust" may surprise you; but I am pretty well tired of this curious drama of earthly life, and would be glad of a change of scene. All my dark views of this poor diseased humanity of ours have been more or less deepened by the scenes I witness here; for altho' I am cut away from the main body of patients, I cannot help coming across sometimes some poor fellow being rolled in on a trolley to the operation theatre; and I cannot help hearing the nurses talking of gruesome things which they have to witness amongst a hundred patients. The bright spot in all this mystery of human suffering is the faith and patience of the afflicted; and the almost superlative kindness of the nurses and some of the doctors. I think women are nearer to heaven than we are. At least, their love and kindness under the most revolting conditions seems a foreshadowing of that Providence that counts the sparrow on the housetops and numbers the hair on our heads. And just as war, hideous as it is, develops all the latent good in our race, so suffering (and it seems universal) seems to call forth all that is divine within us. Someone has said that the invention of the lucifer-match was the greatest achievement of the 19th century. I am of opinion that the match must yield its place of precedence to the establishment of trained and skilled nurses.

I hope you keep well. I am sure you are working hard as ever. Your remarks in your letter of July 5th as to the attitude of the working man towards the capitalist, viewing life spectacularly, and not rationally, have often occurred to me. The vast body of the people have yet to learn what are the real constituents of human happiness; and alas! the whole tendency of modern thought and action is to intensify that universal and ruinous theory that all things have to be measured by their money value, and there is no other. If ever the masses came to understand that money is the meanest and most powerless factor in creating human happiness; and that all the great and good things of life are unpurchasable, things might swing round to an equilibrium. But the brownstone mansion seems such a contrast to the tenement house that reason has no place there.

I shall probably be retained here for some time longer. It would be a great pleasure to hear from you, if your time permits. Meanwhile keep me in your memory. Your friendship is one of the sheet-anchors of life.

Ever affectionately,
dear Dr. Holmes,
P. A. Sheehan

South Infirmary, Cork
Oct. 16, 1912

Dear Dr. Holmes,

I wrote you a few days ago; and the infliction of this second letter is due partly to the superabundant leisure I have at present; but principally to my desire to tell you how pleased I am at the compliments that have lately been paid you. Dear old St. Paul tells us: "Rejoice with them that rejoice"; and to me, it is far the greater pleasure to be able to congratulate my friends than to receive congratulations for myself. That compliment of the President is worth noting; but, of the many others, I sh'd prefer the reception you had at the College, when your degree was conferred. There is a spontaneity in the enthusiasm of the young that makes it very valuable; and you have now not only academic honors; but this unique distinction that you are the only septuagenarian that ever lived who would say that the young lads of the present day are quite equal, if not superior to, our own contemporaries. For myself, I am always the *laudator temporis acti;* I think the world, at least this little section, that makes so much noise in the world, is much degenerated. I hope no whispers of envy will follow these acclamations; for there is a truth in the old saying: *Laudatur, et alget.* There is only one matter which to me is unforgivable in your fine career—that you have not written some great book on history or political economy. I have always thought you could so as well as Bryce[51] or Lecky;[52] and I should like future generations to know you, even as you are known to your contemporaries. I think mysticism is not in your line. I remember you had no sympathy with Emerson; and not much with Carlyle. But you could direct this very practical and erratic generation on your own lines. And, considering the stirring days of your youth, your "Memoirs" would be very valuable to the future.

I am pulling along like a bird with a broken wing; when Death looks in through one window, the doctors order him off, altho' I should like to open the door to him; and then he hovers around trying to get them off their guard. Some day he will succeed.

I have just had a letter from Lady Castletown. Lord C. is much better. They leave for London at the end of the month.

> Always affectionately and
> sincerely,
> P. A. Sheehan

Supreme Court of the
United States
Washington, D. C.
Oct. 18, 1912

My dear friend,

Your letter gives me the heart ache. I have been thinking so much about you and hoping so much for good news. I wrote from Beverly Farms to you a letter that you seem not to have received, directed to Doneraile. Of course I agree with your dislike of money as an ideal, a domination for which I fear the upper strata of the world are more responsible for than the lower,—but unlike you I should not express my dislike in terms of morality. It seems to me that a general fact rather is to be regarded like a physical phenomenon—accepted like any other phenomenon so far as it exists—to be combated or got around so far as may be, if one does not like it, as soon as fully possible. I always say yes—whatever is, is right—but not necessarily will be for thirty seconds longer. I don't know whether I ever mentioned my impressions from rereading Plato—that it was the first articulate assertion of the superiority of the internal life. This summer I was interested to see this point of view more fully developed and no less keenly felt by Epictetus. And if you find yourself able to read books, I got the greatest pleasure from Zimmern's[53] Greek Commonwealth (Oxford, Clarendon Press, 1911) which contrasts strikingly our modern ideal of comfort with that of the Greeks who knew little of it but built the Parthenon and did all the other wonderful things. I feel like repeating to you Hamlet's

"Absent thee from felicity a while"—you give such comfort and joy to one at least who loves you. I am old though I can't realize it, and I hope you will stick it out as long as I do, to help in maintaining the high hearted feeling about this life. I tend towards gloomy views from time to time, but set it down partly to age—and partly content myself by reflecting that I am not running the universe—and am not called on to lie awake with cosmic worries. I took great comfort this summer from Fabre's[54] Souvenirs Entomologiques, and his most charming pictures of maggots preparing the way for a destiny they did not understand. If the maggots, why not man? As you know I don't express this in your terms. I don't even speak of purposes or designs which for all I know are inadequate to the foundation of all, but I am content to believe that probably I do not see the ultimate significance of things (to speak in human terms) and to crack at it, without inquiring too curiously what if any that ultimate significance may be. My dear friend, this abstract discourse seems heartless when you are ill, but I talk on, hoping to give you a moment's distraction, not that I am not thinking of you all the time. I know something of the terrible side of the hospital at second hand. My own experiences are far off and of a time and circumstance when one took things somewhat brutally. I hope you soon may escape those sights. Meantime be sure of my constant affection.

Yours as always,
O. W. Holmes

Supreme Court of the
United States
Washington, D. C.
October 27, 1912

My dear friend,

Your second letter has just arrived and I hasten to add a postscript to my answer to your former one. By the by, I have doubted whether you received all my letters but to the best of my memory I never have let a week go by without writing when I have heard from you. You doubt if mysticism is in my line—and you are right if mysticism means belief in an ineffable direct intercourse with the higher powers. Yet I used to say, and still might, that every wise man is a mystic at bottom. That is, he recognizes the probability that his ultimates are not cosmic ultimates. . . . You put it much too strongly when you say that I had no sympathy with Emerson. When he was breaking and I was still young, I saw him on the other side of the street and ran over and said to him: "If I ever do anything, I shall owe a great deal of it to you," which was true. He was one of those who set one on fire—to impart a [thought] was the gift of genius. My qualification is that I don't regard either him or Carlyle as thinkers. They are at the opposite pole—poets—whose function is not to discern but to make us realize truth. My father once asked me what book I would take to a desert island if I could have but one. I said The French Revolution. I should not say so now, but that wish indicated my appreciation of his [Carlyle's] imaginative power and his humor. And I should be inclined to add that he reached the highest point in the language in the magnificence of his prose. I don't care what he thinks—because I don't regard thinking as his job. You make me talk about myself in defence of an ideal that I have passionately followed. Don't talk about me going into other fields, to which I have not given the study of a life. As a fellow once said to me about cigars: Only the first rate lasts. The only thing that charms my fancy is to know a thing as a master and to put into it some fundamental ideas, that the public won't know enough to give you credit for—that you are lucky if you get any credit for it, but that if your dream is true [your ideas] are first rate and shaping. Then to carry your theory and attitude into detail and practice and thus to submit it to the test of reality is the other half. But is not the big thing to show the infinite in the finite? to take some detail that presents itself as mere arbitrary fact and to show it as a case of the universal? I confess that most of Bryce's [writings] (we have been friends from youth) seems to me diluted with industry. He has poured so constantly that there has been no time for the crystallization of genius. So far as I know Lecky, I should say, moreover the same thing—although I think he had a most aggravating gift for being right when men with more lightning in them are so often wrong.

Dear friend, again understand that I write about other things than yourself only because I hope I may amuse or distract you.

Ever yours affectionately,
O. W. Holmes

Supreme Court of the
United States
Washington, D. C.
November 23, 1912

My dear friend,

Your new story came a few days ago. I have begun it and am impatient to read more as soon as the stress of work permits. There is a slight anxiety in writing you for fear that you don't receive my letters. If you could get some one to send a line just saying that the two I have sent as I shall send this to the South Infirmary are received, I should feel freer in snatching a moment when I can send you my love. I have just made up my mind that I can not go to Richmond and Petersburg tomorrow for the funeral of the wife of a friend of mine, an old Confederate officer, and it has reminded me that I am of the age when one must be prepared for one's self and one's dearest—yet I can't feel so. Life still seems vigorous both in my wife and me. I only hope to meet the inevitable like a philosopher when it comes.

Let me turn to more cheerful themes, though I must add that at those moments when one fleetingly feels as if one has done one's work nobly and adequately, death doesn't seem so hard. But whenever for a minute and a half I feel cocky and as if I had done the trick, I at once begin to anticipate the revenge of fate and expect to get jolly well taken down within twenty-four hours. It must be so as long as one is taking part in the fight. I was sorry for Taft in the recent election, and I apprehend trouble from what the Democrats may do with the tariff. I think that probably Taft was the best man, but he made every political mistake—from the beginning when he put Democrats and doubtful Republicans in his cabinet. I said of the Roosevelt movement that it seemed characterized by a strenuous vagueness that made an atmospheric disturbance but transmitted no message. To prick the sensitive points of the social consciousness when one ought to know that the suggestion of cures is humbug, I think wicked.[55]

I have been writing away at decisions. One of the queer aspects of duty is when one is called on to sustain or enforce laws that one believes to be economically wrong and do more harm than good—but as I think we know very little as to what the laws pronounced good; as there is no even, inarticulate agreement as to the ideal to be striven for, and no adequate scientific evidence that this rather than that will tend to bring it about, if we did agree as to what we want, I settle down on simple tests. I look at it like going to the theatre—if you can pay for your ticket and are sure you want to go, I have nothing to say. But I think the crowd would not want what they now do, if they saw further into the facts.

Dear friend, I talk at random, and I fear this ill suits the atmosphere of a sick room, but as I can't see and don't know exactly how or where you are, I fire away, and simply follow my pen, hoping that it may give you a moment's distraction. Whatever I write about it is merely a roundabout way of saying I am thinking of and with you and of sending you my love.

Affectionately yours,
O. W. Holmes

Doneraile, Co. Cork
December 2, 1912

Dear Dr. Holmes,

Just at this moment, sitting at "my ain fireside," your letter was put into my hands. I have two or more correspondents whose handwriting on the envelope gives me cold chills all over; and a few, which I open with anticipation of pleasure. Amongst these latter, yours holds first place; and I always open your letter with the exclamation: "Not forgotten!"

I made a dash for liberty last Monday week. One of the doctors was holding out against me to the last; but he was finally persuaded that hospital life was not good from my standpoint; and so I packed up, and got back once more amongst my books and papers, and the kind faces of friends. All here have been exceedingly kind without distinction of class or creed; and altho' I begged and prayed that there should be no demonstration, I am afraid I shall have to face the band and illuminations tomorrow night. Poor people! they insisted on it; and it would be churlish to refuse any little testimony of their affection.

I do not know what you will think of "Miriam Lucas."[56] It carries out my pet theory that there is an equilibrium in human life—some compensation or balance that, in the end, makes the poor somewhat nearer to real happiness than the rich. I have seen both sides of the big question; and so far as mere happiness is concerned, I think on the whole the poor have the best of it, at least in this Ireland of ours. I am never tired of quoting a story by A. K. H. B. (The Country Parson)[57] in one of his books—the Grampian shepherd, coming home after a day's honest work, and declaring, after he had changed his boots, and swallowed a wholesome supper, and taken up *Chambers' Journal:*

"I do not envy the Duke of Buccleuch;" and, as a contrast, the mono-maniac in his ducal mansion above the Thames, shouting impatiently:

"Oh, that river, that river, always rolling and rolling, and never rolling away!"

I see that the *N. York Herald* and another American paper hint that in the 3rd book of "M. Lucas" I write "in complete ignorance of the conditions of life in N. York." I should like to know where the picture fails. It is not flattering, but I wrote after making careful inquiries amongst friends who have visitied here from time to time. But I perceive that nations have nerves as well as individuals; and altho' I thought we Irish had a double dose of them, I perceive that the malady is universal.

Don't speak of death. Death is not for you for many years to come. I wish the President[58] would make you Ambassador at St. James's, or at Paris. But I suppose a Democratic Government will keep the plums for its own. I believe this party politics is the one great curse of mankind. It has paralysed everything here; and stifles all genius and original talent. And I suspect it is the same the wide world over.

If too early to wish you a happy Xmas, it is never premature to wish you every blessing, temporal and spiritual.

Always affectionately,
P. A. Sheehan

Supreme Court of the
United States
Washington, D. C.
December 15, 1912

Dear Canon,

It is a joy to see your handwriting as firm as ever and to see the
heading, Doneraile. As to your "not forgotten" I don't believe you doubt
that you never are very long out of my mind. I must tell you before I forget to mention it that two ladies whom I frequent (at the rare odd moments
when I have a chance to call) are great admirers of *Under The Cedars and
the Stars,* and always inquire about you. I have been so very hard at work
that I read nothing and so haven't finished M. Lucas. This last week, for
instance, besides sitting in Court 4 hours each day, except Saturday which
is Conference and more fatiguing, I have written 2 decisions to be delivered
tomorrow, had to be ready at yesterday's Conference to vote on about 50
cases, including those argued, and dined out nearly every night. I like to
work at high pressure, but it leaves time for nothing else, as I neither work
nor read after dinner. I do so like to think of the band and illuminations
for your return. I don't wonder they all love you—one doesn't have to be
of your parish for that.

Again to interrupt, lest I forget, don't bother about writing except
to let me know once in a while that my letters are received, unless you
feel like it. I will try to slip in a letter to you between cases from time to
time, irrespective of answers.

Last Sunday, Dec. 8, my ten years since I took my seat were up, and
I am now free to retire when I like. But (apropos of some suggestions of
yours) while only the philosophical side of things interests me I don't care
to write except on subjects which I think I know to the bottom, and therefore I think it wise, while my powers seem unabated, to try to put a touch
of the infinite into the law, rather than turn to other fields. That sounds
rather swaggery, but if I have succeeded at all, what I have aimed at through-
out has been to exhibit the particular in the light of the universal, so far as
may be. . . .Here I was interrupted for luncheon and after it I find the usual
little slip from the Chief Justice allotting decisions to be written. I have
two and shall have to bestir myself. You say you wish the President would
make me Ambassador. English friends sometimes used to suggest that years

ago, but even when I was a judge in Massachusetts I wouldn't have taken it—very much less would I take it now. That is not a career; my work is—to give it up in order to be an ornamental umbrella handle! No thank you. But people differ so. Last night at dinner at Justice Hughes's,[59] McKenna[60] (of our bench and a Catholic) evidently thought, indeed, I believe, said, that four years of the Presidency was worth a life on the bench. To which I replied that to my mind, 4 years on the Bench was worth a lifetime in the Presidency. I then said to Senator Root[61] (who you may remember has been Secy of State, etc., etc.) that I never had regarded any office as an object and he said neither had he. I think he meant it and I know that I did. I have told you of our Regimental Surgeon's distinction of external and internal men. I don't see how any internal man can regard an office as anything but an incidental advantage (when it is one). The thing I have wanted to do and want to do is to put as many new ideas into the law as I can, to show how particular solutions involve general theory, and to do it with style. I should like to be admitted to be the greatest jurist in the world, but I wouldn't do much more than walk across the street to be called Chief Justice instead of Justice—though I think the difference has affected the present incumbent. I no longer hear him wishing that he could retire! You see, I talk ahead just as usual, hoping that you will prefer that to conversation on the invalid footing—but I am thinking of you always with constant affection.

O. W. Holmes.

I am with you so far as I can judge about the relative happiness of the poor. My wife was making the same remark just as your letter came.

Doneraile, Co. Cork
Jan. 20, 1913

My dear Dr. Holmes,

A sentence in your last letter (dated, to my shame, Dec. 15, 1912) makes me half timid in writing you. I pictured you to myself, as all day long in a stuffy court, listening to evidence and appeal, the harangues of barristers making special pleas, the testimony of witnesses more or less credible; and then enduring that most severe of all moral strains, the balancing of data & arguments and the forming a conscientious judgment on knotty and difficult points of fact and law; and I said: Is it right or fair that after such a day's work, that Judge Holmes should sit down & write a long and interesting letter to an old parish priest in a remote Irish village, instead of burying himself in an armchair and giving his mind every repose? And I resolved that I should write and write regularly in order to keep up a chain of correspondence that is so precious; but I shall order the Judge, that under all pains and penalties, that he must only write during vacation terms, when he has abundunt leisure. Yet, I want you to understand that in a pretty extensive correspondence, there is only one address that makes me jump, and that is your handwriting. Let me add, that I think I have received all your letters. They are carefully filed and kept to be disposed at your pleasure when I shall have gone.

There was another remark in your last letter, that showed how deeply interested you are in your great profession, altho' it depressed me somewhat to reflect how difficult it is to secure a great position as a jurist. Probably I am speaking from inexperience, because so few, so very few legal men have left a permanent reputation behind them in these countries. The great English judges are hardly dead when they are forgotten; and what is more strange, whilst this generation reads with some pleasure great judicial charges of a hundred years ago, no one cares about contemporaries. Lord Russell became famous for his splendid cross-examinations & final address in the Parnell trial; but no one minded him as Chief Justice. Our Chief Justice (Palles)[62] is known in legal circles as a profound student of law; but his reputation is limited to the Law Courts in Dublin. But I suppose all this is true of every profession. Is it the general levelling up or the general levelling down of this Democratic age that makes remarkable men almost impossible? And nothing has astonished me more than the manner in which obscure and partly illiterate men in the States, such as Lincoln, Grant, etc., developed such tremendous powers and became "leaders of men." I have just been reading W. Churchill's "Crisis"[63] and got a larger idea of these men than ever before. I can forgive Walt Whitman a good deal for "Captain! Oh, my Captain!"[64]

There! I have scarcely left space to wish you a most prosperous and happy N. Year, full of good, noble work, and rich in all manner of blessings.

Always sincerely
my dear Dr. Holmes,
P. A. Sheehan

Washington, D. C.
Jan. 31, 1913

My dear Friend,

Your letter came this morning and started the day with a glow. I *have* been under such intense pressure of work that I haven't kept my promise to write regardless of answers but today I know that our usual Saturday Conference is postponed to Monday and I shall have plenty of time to do what remains to be done—so everything concurs—but that you may see that what I say is true. I have written three decisions this week (in the day time, as I don't work at night) besides going to the capital and sitting 4 hours each day. We don't listen to testimony, as ordinarily we deal only with questions of law, but that means the work is harder and more intense. I should say, in answer to some of your reflections, that what has happened is not loosening but specializing—so that people, unless like you they address and charm a general public, get their recognition from other specialists. I don't remember whether I ever quoted to you a talk I had with the late Alex. Agassiz.[65] I said to him—You write a brochure about something that I never heard of and then a man in London and another at St. Petersburg, and a chap in Milan and another in Paris say that this is first class; and you say, I have achieved a European reputation and are satisfied. And he said, Yes. I feel much the same way. I like to have the Bar think well of me, but the only thing I care much for is what a few masters scattered here and there say. I often think not without sadness of the profound difference in the interest of my friend the Chief Justice[66] and myself—so profound that I never talk about my half. He is always thinking what will be the practical effect of the decision (which of course is the ultimate justification of condemnation of the principle adopted.) I think of its relation to the theory and philosophy of the law—if that isn't too pretentious a way of putting it. We generally come out the same way by very different paths. But we sometimes come together head on with a whack. By the by, I have just received a notice of the German translation of my book written in Norwegian or some unknown tongue and I can't guess whether it skins me or anoints my head with oil,—rather aggravating? You speak of Walt Whitman. I came to him late, but I came all right. He and the starling are the two creatures that can produce symphonic effects by a sequence of sounds. Did you ever read "Out of the cradle endlessly rocking" or Song of the Banner at Daybreak— or for simple pathos, "Come up from the Fields Father"? I am pretty sure you would come down, if you did. Apropos of your Canyon in the Sierras there was a Chicago novel called the Cliff Dwellers—if I remember rightly— that embodied the same idea in its title. I never heard of it giving offense to anyone. But as you say, all nations are sensitive, not the least the English who call themselves thick skinned. Hawthorne showed it, when he made some comments, I have forgotten what.

I grieve to think that you have days of pain—dear me, if I stopped to think of the suffering in the world, I couldn't work. I do hope that doing all one can, makes up for not stopping. One must stop when the sufferer is a beloved friend, but everything, even pain, seems so transitory to me. I take comfort in thinking of Fabre's grubs that prepare a dwelling for the beetles that they are to become and never see. I say to myself man also may have cosmic destinies beyond his ken. But I fear that I am repeating what I have said before. The collateral trouble of intense work is that one's mind does not relax easily into the free spontaneity of letter writing. In the back of one's head is some case, or a correction that should be made in a proof that the printer has, etc., etc. In a moment I must go to Court. This is not much good for all my fair beginning, but it will take you my love. . . .

Affectionately yours,
O. W. Holmes

Washington, D. C.
Feb. 5, 1913

My dear Canon,

This is a postscript, just to tell you that the evening after my letter went, a neighboring lady came to us dilating with delight in *Under the Cedars and the Stars,* which another admirer of yours whom I had made acquainted with the book—(she had read others of yours) had lent to her. So the good work goes on. We have adjourned for three weeks. I have only three cases to write, and a dinner in N. Y. to go to on the 15th where contrary to all my habits I make a speech. So I hope for some leisure but. . . .

not yet. I think of you a great deal and am always hoping that you may not be suffering.

Affectionately yours,
O. W. Holmes

Doneraile, Co. Cork
February 25, 1913

Dear Dr. Holmes,

I was just about to write to you to ask the favor of a newspaper cutting of your speech in New York, when the coveted article reached my hands. It is just what I expected—terse with thought. Your auditors if they followed you with intelligent interest, must have carefully abstained from champagne. But then you must know that you have spoken not a speech but a book.

A kind friend was good enough to pay me the compliment lately of saying (he is an organist) that my books are like Wagneric music—they must be read three or four times before one can understand them. However accurate that may be, I can say it truly of your speech. As I went over and over the sentences I said—that idea needs pages to develop. There is a tremendous truth hidden away in the chrysalis of a few words. I notice the same circumstances in all your speeches. How absolutely original they must have sounded at the banquet; and what a dainty morceau [morsel] they must be to the studious epicure of the library. I like too the glints of poetry here and there; and if I can not share in your sunny optimism (because I think it is the individual and not nations, or races, we have to study that develop) at least it is charming to hear the Alpine shepherds calling to each other across their desolate valleys.

My health continues poor enough, days of relief alternating with days of pain and discomfort. I find a consolation in thinking how much worse I might be; and contrasting my infirmities with those of others. "It is a sad world, my merry masters."

I find I gave some offense in New York in Book III of "Miriam Lucas." Yet I can not perceive that I said anything but what may be said of all great cities. But I notice how sensitive are whole nations, as well as individuals. My books have never caught on in France because I have written somewhat enthusiastically about Germany; but in the Fatherland & especially in Austro-Hungary, these books are great favourites. I think it was the curious remark made by Whistler, or some other artist, that modern N. York with its skyscrapers resembled nothing so much as a canyon in the Sierras that set the teeth of my American friends on edge. I should not like to be thought capable of wilful offense there; because, like many other authors, it was to American appreciation that was mainly due the success of my books.

Adieu! All blessings be with you.

Thanks for all your letters which came in quick and welcome succession; and which must have consumed much of your precious time.

Your name turned up a few days ago, when Lord & Lady Castletown called here. Her Ladyship was wondering whether you would pay the Green Isle a visit this year. We are in the throes of expectation about the Home Rule Bill. It will be the best for England; the worst for Ireland since the Act of Union.

> Prospere procedet.
> Always affectionately,
> P. A. Sheehan

> Washington, D. C.
> March 9, 1913

My dear Canon,

Your dear letter arrived as a birthday present to me, for yesterday I turned 72! So I shall take part of this letter in telling you of the momentous doings on that day. In the morning we had to make our official call on the new President.[67] I have my apprehensions about him, but at least he can speak English, has the manners of a man of the world, and let us out pretty soon (after a whisper in his ear from the Captain on duty which probably told him that we couldn't go till he gave the word!)

Then after leaving cards on the Vice President[68] we went down to our Saturday Conference. Then at luncheon time, I having let out without malice that it was my birthday, the Chief Justice produced two bottles of champagne and we derogated from our habits by drinking wine in the middle of the day. When I got home I found flowers and flowers—from one of my brethren and from one or two ladies—I know not—and letters and telegrams to be answered as far as may be till dinner time. Then we had some pleasant people, Jusserand[69] the French Ambassador and his wife among others, and he gave me another surprize by making a little speech and proposing my health. So if alcohol will do it, I ought to be pretty well. I did not make a reply speech—it seemed too much of a good thing. Again a lot of flowers arranged by my wife and truly beautiful, coupled with good victuals, though I say it. The men always like my library, where they go to smoke as is the habit here after dinner, and everybody was so pleasant and friendly. Gen'l Wood,[70] the Chief of Staff, and his wife, both of whom I like very much, and George Vanderbilt,[71] a man of taste, a lover of books, and I should think of simple, virtuous habits, with his handsome, intelligent wife, and others [were there]. There was talk of Roosevelt suing a paper for libel apropos of his habits.[72] Seemingly Wood had been asked what he would say about it and had answered that he never saw R. drink any spirits. And when reminded that, yes, once he did—when notified at tennis that Taft had been nominated—he said that was such good news that they must have a drink. The irony of time! That last phrase makes me think of Fate and so of Jean Christophe[73]—have you read it? I took a volume in the train and read a little and found in it a terrible sentence—"aux yeux du chaos qui luisent a travers le voile de l'orde." It reminded me of an old sentence of my own that I didn't quite dare repeat to your beloved and holy ears. Oh dear, I hope I don't deceive you in any way about myself. I don't mean to and should be quite ready to have you see all my inside works if they could be made visible. By the by, Bergson,[74] the philosopher, was lecturing in N. Y. when I was there, but I did not see him. I found his writing very stimulating in the way that many things are that one doesn't believe. But as I don't believe his message very much, I less regretted our not meeting. Well, this comes pretty close to a letter of pure gossip doesn't it? but it takes you my love.

Affectionately yours,
O. W. Holmes

My dear Canon,

Another delightful letter from you. I had imagined that I should be
the writer this season, without return, until you should feel thoroughly
ready to make it, and lo, you have been better than I. You speak of Bergson
—he was delighting the ladies of New York when I was there, but as my
stay was only one day and two halves I didn't see him. I read his books two
years ago and take pleasure in telling enthusiasts that he was anticipated
nearly a century by Rejected Address—"Thinking is but an idle waste of
thought"—you remember the Byron one. He is stimulating but generally
speaking I don't believe him. I don't even believe his science, although in-
competent to contradict it. His criticism of the Greek philosophy at the
end of Creative Evolution I thought very suggestive. But he spends a lot of
intellect to show that intellect is only a practical tool inside of life and inadequate on speculative themes. I couldn't see that he made out that it was
not the best thing we have. He got one motif, I suspect, from the delightful
adorable Fabre—Souvenirs Entomologiques—of whom no doubt I wrote to
you in the summer. Fabre is a stout old anti-Darwinian and heaps up evidence of immediate vision of what to do—quite different from intellect—in
insects, coupled with hopeless stupidity as soon as they are off the track of
their instinct. I think he would delight you, and there are 10 vols. which
can be read in anywhere for half an hour and yet which are profitable in
sequence. In the last vol. of Jean Christophe, Bergson and my old friend
Wm James[75] are spoken of as a sort of holiday taken by the human mind
after the work at high pressure that it has been doing. I certainly can't bring
my mind to believe that either of them has advanced speculation very much
except perhaps as an extreme protest against Hegel's attempt to make a
syllogism wag its tail, or, more plainly, to get life out of logic chopping
(this without prejudice to W. James's psychology). But nowadays I am all
in law—I eat and drink it with occasional alarums and excursions in the
form of dinner or a call upon some agreeable woman, and a semi-occasional
letter like this. The thing I sent you from Chaucer my wife had printed for
Easter purposes. Our spring is roaring in upon us with cataracts of flowers.
There are so many large flowering trees and shrubs that the panorama from

the first magnolias in March to the laurel at the end of May is splendid—really adequate enough to satisfy me. I read no newspapers and can't talk politics, but I think our people are intent on trying how much uneconomic expenditure the country will bear. I regard the anti-trust legislation that I help to enforce idiotic, and I fear that the prospective changes in the tariff mean widespread ruin if the Democrats stick to their program. Our people as yet seem not to have grasped the thought that public wealth is consistent with private ownership. I touched on that in my speech, which Senator Lodge had printed as a public document, though how far it was circulated by that means I don't know. I hope that your periods of suffering have ceased. I think much about you. I have not yet decided whether it will be possible for me to get abroad this year. If I do I shall hope to see you but everything is still in the air.

Yours affectionately,
O. W. Holmes

36, Grosvenor Road
Westminster
June 20, 1913

My beloved Canon,

If nothing busts we shall meet! I haven't dared to write to you until I thought it pretty certain—but I am just replying to Lady Castletown that I shall come there after the season here has ended. My doubt has been whether I ought to burden her, and I suggested going to Cork and motoring over—but she says come. Tell me if you know whether I ought not to. I can tell you of some admirers of yours that I introduced to your writings. I leave the above address on Monday and go to Rt. Hon'ble Sir F. Pollock, 21 Hyde Park Place, for a week or more—after that or at any time care of Morgan, Grenfell & Co. 22 Old Broad Street, London, always will reach me.

With anticipation
Affectionately yours,
O. W. Holmes

Doneraile, Co. Cork
June 21, 1913

Dear Dr. Holmes,

It was only yesterday that Lord Castletown told me you were in London, and that they were expecting you this month or next. This is a delightful piece of news, I am distinctly of the opinion that your visit to the Castletowns would not only be a pleasure to them; but would raise Lord Castletown's spirits a good deal. He is much improved; and I am sure if his solitude were broken by a visit from you, it would help him much. I think they have none, or few visitors just now, and we have Irish weather, variable, but charming.

Need I say what a ray of sunshine your visit will cast over a broken life like mine?

Always affectionately &
Sincerely,
P. A. Sheehan

Notes

1. Oliver Wendell Holmes, Jr., *Speeches,* (Boston, 1891).
2. Patrick Augustine Sheehan, *Under the Cedars and the Stars,* (Dublin, 1901). This was a collection of observations, thoughts and reflections.
3. Holmes moved into his new house on Lafayette Square in Washington, D. C. in December, 1902.
4. Bernard Edward Barnaby Fitz-Patrick, 2nd Baron, (1849-1937). Soldier, M. P., Chancellor of the Royal University of Ireland.
5. Edward Douglas White (1845-1921), Associate Justice of the United States Supreme Court, 1894-1910, Chief Justice, 1910-1921.
6. Melville D. Fuller (1833-1910), Chief Justice of the United States Supreme Court, 1888-1910.
7. Northern Securities Case (1904), a celebrated early decision in which Holmes participated. Though Holmes had a reputation as a liberal, he confounded the President, Theodore Roosevelt, and the public by voting in the minority to deny the application of the Sherman Anti-Trust Act to a railroad corporation involved in the suit. He based his decision on the evolutionary proposition that corporations will naturally grow in size and complexity, quite without regard to statute law.
8. Hon. Ursula Emily Clare St. Leger, Lady Castletown, (d. 1927), daughter of the 4th Viscount Doneraile. The Castletowns lived at Doneraile Court, Co. Cork. Originally part of the estate of Edmund Spenser, the Elizabethan poet, the land came into possession of the St. Leger family who built the Court, designed by William Rothery about 1730.
9. Matthew Arnold (1822-1888), English poet whose revolt against Victorian materialism appealed to Sheehan.
10. Arthur Hugh Clough (1819-1861), English poet with whom Sheehan had much in common: deep inner conflicts, and admiration for both Carlyle and Emerson, for example.
11. Alfred Lord Tennyson (1809-1892), English poet, too facile for Sheehan's taste.
12. James Russell Lowell (1819-1891), American poet and editor who was especially appreciated in the British Isles because of his defense of American literature before foreigners.
13. Sir John Everett Millais (1829-1896), English painter.
14. John Ruskin (1819-1900), English critic and social theorist to whom Holmes may have taken exception because of his anti-Darwinian attitudes.
15. Algernon Charles Swinburne (1837-1909), English poet and something of a favorite of Canon Sheehan.

16. Salomon Reinach (1858-1932), French archaeologist.
17. Battle during the American Civil War, September 17, 1862.
18. *Lisheen,* (Dublin, 1907), a novel of life in Ireland which includes Sheehan's lament over the abandonment of Ireland on the part of young men and women bound for America.
19. *Parerga,* (London, 1908), a sequel to *Under the Cedars and the Stars.*
20. *Lisheen.*
21. Sir (William Matthew) Flinders Petrie (1853-1942), English archaeologist and Egyptologist.
22. James Bryce (1832-1922), British historian, statesman, diplomat; H. M. Ambassador to the United States, 1907-1913.
23. Sir Antony Patrick McDonnell (1844-1925), Under-Secretary of State for Ireland, 1902-1908.
24. Mrs. John Richard Green (Alice Stopford Green), (1848-1928), historian.
25. Sir Leslie Scott (1869-1950), British judge and politician.
26. British Association (for the Advancement of Science). Established in 1841, partly as a forum for scientists to discuss their work and partly as a means for presenting scientific findings to the public.
27. *American Ecclesiastical Review,* founded in 1899 by Rev. Herman J. Heuser (1852-1933), later the biographer of Canon Sheehan.
28. Augustin Eugene Scribe (1791-1861), French dramatist and librettist.
29. *Tractus de Legibus* (1612), a treatise on law by Francisco Suarez (1548-1617) in which a systematic exposition of a legal code stressed the voluntary element.
30. Sir Edward Coke (1552-1634), English jurist.
31. Sir Thomas Lyttleton (1422?-1481), English jurist. Sheehan may have intended by the phrase "Coke on Lyttleton" a reference to Coke's commentaries on Lyttleton.
32. Thomas Carlyle (1795-1881), English writer, author of *Sartor Resartus,* (New York, 1913), p. 132.
33. Probably *The Future in America,* (London, 1906) by H. G. Wells (1866-1946), English author.
34. *Times Literary Supplement,* Aug. 26, 1909 (No. 398). The leading article notes the centenary of the birth of Oliver Wendell Holmes, pp. 305-06. The letters of Swinburne mentioned are reviewed in the TLS, June 3, 1909 (No. 386), p. 204. The reference to Patmore may have been based on his reference to Longfellow's poetry as "such heaps of slush." See Basil Champneys, *Coventry Patmore Memoirs and Correspondence,* 2 vols. (London, 1900), II, p. 182.
35. *The Intellectuals,* (London, 1910), fictionalized discussions among Irish intellectual club members looking to political and social improvements in Ireland.
36. Robert Hugh Benson (1871-1914), English Catholic convert, writer, and apologist. The article referred to is "Catholicism and the Future," *The Atlantic Monthly,* CVI (1910), pp. 166-75.

37. Melville D. Fuller

38. In Catholic parlance, adoption of a critical approach to the Bible, rejection of the intellectualism of scholastic philosophy and theology, with a corresponding subordination of doctrine and the teaching authority of the Church. Condemned by Pius X in his encyclical, *Pascendi* (1907).

39. Pierre Loti, pseud. for Julian Viaud (1850-1923), French novelist. Loti's insistence on viewing all of Nature as one piece, with animals as well as men as part of Nature's expression, is the source of Sheehan's objections.

40. Joris Karl Huysman (1848-1907), French novelist of a Dutch family. *En Route* (1895) is a fictional account of Huysman's return to the Catholic church.

41. Sir Frederick E. Pollock (1845-1937), English legal scholar and an intimate of Holmes.

42. Charles Francis Keary (1848-1917), *The Pursuit of Reason,* (Cambridge, 1910).

43. University of Berlin (1910) and the University of Oxford (1909).

44. John Henry Cardinal Newman (1801-1890), English author and theologian. Catholic convert.

45. Holmes, "The Class of '61, at the 50th Anniversary of Graduation, June 28, 1911," *Speeches,* (Boston, 1934), pp. 95-99.

46. Tennyson, *In Memoriam,* XCVI; Conclusion, st. xxxvi.

47. *Queen's Fillet,*(London, 1911), a romance set in the days of the French Revolution which contained Sheehan's implicit warning against the dangers of radicalism.

48. *Jerusalem Delivered,* (1575), by Torquato Tasso (1540-1595); Edward Fairfax (1580-1635), English translator.

49. Thomas Edward Brown (1830-1897), English poet who wrote in the Manx dialect.

50. Pierre Joseph Proudhon (1809-1865), French social theorist.

51. James Bryce.

52. William E. H. Lecky (1838-1903). English historian, highly regarded as both stylist and historian.

53. Sir Alfred Eckhard Zimmern (1879-1957), English classical historian.

54. Jean Henri Fabre (1823-1915), French entomologist.

55. 1912 Presidential election in which Taft, the incumbent, was defeated; Theodore Roosevelt's Bull Moose party split the Republicans, leading to their downfall.

56. *Miriam Lucas,* (London, 1912), a novel of an Irish girl's troubles in Ireland and America.

57. Andrew Kennedy Hutchinson Boyd (1825-1899), Scottish Presbyterian divine whose writings included *The Critical Essays of a Country Parson,* (London, 1865).

58. Woodrow Wilson (1856-1924), President of the United States, 1913-1921.

[69]

59. Charles Evans Hughes (1862-1948), Associate Justice of the Supreme Court, 1910-1916, Chief Justice, 1930-1941.
60. Joseph McKenna (1843-1926), Associate Justice of the Supreme Court of the United States, 1898-1925.
61. Elihu Root (1845-1937), American statesman.
62. Sir Christopher Palles (1831-1910), Lord Chief Baron of the Exchequer in Ireland.
63. Winston Churchill (1871-1947), American novelist; *The Crisis* was published in 1901.
64. Walt Whitman (1819-1892), American poet, who wrote the poem in honor of Lincoln, "O Captain! My Captain!"
65. Alexander Agassiz (1835-1910), American marine biologist.
66. Edward Douglas White.
67. Woodrow Wilson.
68. Thomas Riley Marshall (1854-1921), Vice-President of the United States, 1913-1921.
69. Jean Jules Jusserand (1855-1932), French diplomat and ambassador to Washington, 1902-1925.
70. Leonard Wood (1860-1927), American general and administrator.
71. George Washington Vanderbilt (1862-1914), American philanthropist.
72. Roosevelt did in fact sue the paper *Iron Ore,* in May, 1913, for accusations as to Roosevelt's excessive use of alcohol. He won the case, the editor of *Iron Ore* being unable to produce any witnesses to support his charge.
73. *Jean-Christophe,* a ten volume novel (1904-1910) written by Romain Rolland (1866-1944).
74. Henri Bergson (1859-1941), French philosopher to whose intuitive metaphysics Holmes doubtless objected. One of his well known works was *Creative Evolution.*
75. William James (1842-1910), American philosopher and psychologist who had been a friend of Holmes.